Love Notes: for a Politics of Love

GW00585147

Love Notes

— *for a Politics of Love* —

Philip McKibbin

Lantern Books ● New York
A Division of Booklight Inc.

2019
Lantern Books
128 Second Place
Brooklyn, NY 11231
www.lanternbooks.com

Printed in the United States of America

Names: McKibbin, Philip, author.
Title: Love notes : for a politics of love / Philip McKibbin.
Description: Brooklyn, NY : Lantern Books, 2019. | Includes
bibliographical references.
Identifiers: LCCN 2019009843 (print) | LCCN 2019019405
(ebook) | ISBN 9781590565896 (ebook) | ISBN 9781590565889
(pbk. : alk. paper)
Subjects: LCSH: Love—Philosophy. | Interpersonal relations—
Moral and ethical aspects. | Nature—Effect of human beings on.
Classification: LCC BD436 (ebook) | LCC BD436 .M376 2019
(print) | DDC 128/.46—dc23
LC record available at https://lccn.loc.gov/2019009843

to all those who are working for a better world

Contents

Introduction

Thank you for picking up this book. I am glad it has reached you.

You may be wondering what the Politics of Love is. I want to share some of my thinking with you, but let me begin by saying this: I am still exploring the Politics of Love. The ideas in this book are simply a beginning. . . .

Max Harris and I first sketched the Politics of Love in 2015, in an article we published on The Aotearoa Project, a blog on politics, culture, and society that focuses on New Zealand. (Aotearoa is the Māori name for our country.) In that piece—which is the first chapter in this collection—we argued that politics can, and should, be more loving. It was, essentially, an expression of our belief that love can be both deeply critical and genuinely constructive. Since then, we have continued to develop the Politics of Love.[1] In December 2018, we held The Politics of Love: A Conference at All Souls College, Oxford, where we brought together thinkers and activists from diverse traditions to discuss this emerging theory.

The Politics of Love is a values-based politics, which affirms the importance of people and extends beyond us to

---

1 For a list of Max Harris's written contributions to the Politics of Love, see the bibliography at the end of this book.

non-human animals and the natural environment. This politics is for everyone: it holds that *all* people are important—and as such, it incorporates a commitment to radical equality. It includes non-human animals, because a politics that did not take non-human animals (and their suffering) into account could not be considered loving. And it encompasses a concern for the natural environment, because it recognises not only that our planet and its ecosystems are important to our well-being, but that they are deserving of love *in themselves*.

Love can be understood as an orientation, or 'attitude'. It is a way of relating: to ourselves, to each other, and to the wider world. The Politics of Love is an actively inclusive framework. I imagine it as a round space, with love at its centre. It celebrates loving values, such as *care*, *concern*, and *commitment*, which derive from, and are held in balance by, love. These values can guide action and inform policy. I follow African American thinker bell hooks, who writes, 'there can be no love when there is domination', and so, I imagine the Politics of Love as anti-racist, anti-sexist, anti-speciesist, and opposed to all forms of domination. Indeed, I understand this intersectional commitment as constituting the outer limits of the space, determining what is and is not loving. The Politics of Love elaborates loving relationship.

The 'space' that the Politics of Love encompasses extends both inwards and outwards: it is an ethic that we can embody, as individuals and as communities, and it is through relationship that we realise it. I see an affinity between the Politics of Love and what angel Kyodo williams has termed 'radical dharma'. She writes:

Each community possesses, as Gandhi offered, a piece of the truth, of Dharma. When we seek the embodiment of these truths, giving ourselves permission to be more honest, more healed, more whole, more complete—when we become radical— neither the path of solely inward-looking liberation nor the pursuit of an externalised social liberation prevails; rather a third space, as-yet-unknown, emerges. It is a radical dharma. And it is ours.

In affirming values such as *listening*, *trust*, and *collaboration*, the Politics of Love endeavours to involve people from diverse backgrounds. We must work to nurture respectful exchange within this space, because otherwise we will not succeed in maintaining it. Importantly, it must involve spokespeople for non-human animals and the natural environment—for those who are, and that which is, incapable of full self-representation.

You are probably wondering what the Politics of Love looks like in practice. You will find many suggestions in this book; a glance at the contents page will give you an idea of the scope of this collection. However, as I say throughout these chapters, I do not have all of the answers. The notion that one of us has, or that a few of us have, exclusive insight into love is at odds with this vision of politics. The Politics of Love involves all of us, and it entreats each of us: it asks us to care—about ourselves, each other, and the world we share. Indeed, this is the first requirement of the Politics of Love. When we truly care, we feel, and—as importantly—we think. When we are all feeling and thinking, we will begin to realise the Politics of Love together. It is not enough simply to feel and think, though: we must also act. The Politics of Love is a radical vision, and so it urges radical change. Martin Luther King, Jr. expressed a similar sentiment when he wrote, 'True compassion is more than flinging a coin to a beggar; it understands that an edifice which produces beggars needs restructuring.'

This book collects both previously published and unpublished pieces. (Around half of them have been published elsewhere, with outlets such as the *Guardian*, *openDemocracy*, and *Renegade Inc.*) It does not represent a definitive account of the Politics of Love; rather, the pieces that comprise it should be read as notes toward the Politics of Love as I envision it. Each has been written as a stand-alone piece and can be read by itself; for this reason, there is some repetition of ideas and examples. This also means that it is not necessary to read them in the order in which they are presented.

I have collected these pieces in the belief that, when they are read together, they suggest what a comprehensive Politics of Love might eventually look like. I have put them in rough chronological order so that, if you do read them consecutively, you will get a sense of how my thinking on love has unfolded. I have tested ideas; I have explored them with other people; and on certain points, I have changed my mind. I suggest that if you do read this book from cover to cover, you think of the ideas within as a sketch. When you get to the end of the book, some of the lines will seem faint, while others will appear much stronger, having been traced several times—and in those darker lines, you will be able to envisage what the theory might look like when it is developed more fully. . . .

The Politics of Love is not 'my' theory; it is for all of us to contribute to and develop. I am presenting this intellectual journey—which includes missteps I have made, and ideas I have moved beyond—in the belief that it will help you to see the Politics of Love, and what I feel is important to it, more clearly. I know that my thinking, like yours, will continue to change. A careful reading of this book will reveal how I have attempted to develop this politics, as well as principles that might guide its future elaboration.

It is my hope that by making myself vulnerable in this way, I am setting an example that those of you who develop the Politics of Love will consider following. It is okay to change your mind, and sometimes it is necessary: intellectual progress has often been waylaid by those who, falsely believing that admitting to having been wrong is a sign of weakness, attempt to justify what, really, they suspect are false conclusions. The Politics of Love requires that we cultivate intellectual humility; this is part of what it is to work together. The pieces in this collection engage with other people's ideas, agreeing and disagreeing with them. When we think with other people— be it the people in our lives, or those we encounter in books or through oral histories—our thinking becomes richer.

I am aware that some readers—you might be one of them—will want a succinct statement of the Politics of Love. For this reason, I am including the text of the presentation I gave at The Politics of Love: A Conference at All Souls College, Oxford as an appendix. In that presentation, I attempted to summarise Max Harris's and my thinking on the theory. I am including it as an appendix rather than a chapter because most of the ideas it contains can be found, often in greater detail, in other parts of this collection. Nonetheless, it represents the most up-to-date account of my thinking on the Politics of Love as of 15 December 2018.

The pieces in this collection were written between 2015 and 2018. It is necessary for me to say a little about the context in which they were written, as contemporary events influenced many of them. Although you will likely be familiar with most of these events, I am aware that for the majority of readers, New Zealand's politics in particular will be unfamiliar.

When Max and I started writing about the Politics of Love, we were deeply troubled by the relentless march of neoliberalism. In Aotearoa New Zealand, the right wing seemed to be entrenched—John Key, leader of the right-wing National Party, had been Prime Minister for close to a decade—and the Left, having fractured, was proving ineffectual. We had seen some signs that love might prevail, as when marriage equality was finally achieved in 2013, but we could not ignore the backdrop of inequality against which that progress took place, with child poverty and homelessness getting steadily worse.

Since then, a lot has happened—both good and bad—and international events more than domestic ones have informed my exploration of the Politics of Love. Some of those are worth highlighting, as they are mentioned in these pieces. In 2017, Australia legalised marriage equality, to the refrain of 'Love wins!' The debate leading up to this inspired one of my first articles. Internationally, terrorism has become more pernicious, with Daesh (also known as ISIS, IS, or the Islamic State) and other groups taking lives and claiming attention. In the West, we have experienced the rise of nationalism, as evidenced in Brexit and the election of Donald Trump to the US presidency. Alarmingly, action on climate change has slackened: the past four years have been a series of missed opportunities, and have brought us to the very edge of catastrophe.

There has been resistance, though. The Black Lives Matter movement has strengthened, prompting many of us to think critically about racism. We have also witnessed the #MeToo movement, which has called attention to how much work remains to be done for women and girls especially. And consciousness around environmental issues continues to grow.

At home in Aotearoa New Zealand, things have improved . . . somewhat. In the most recent general election, the Green Party campaigned on love. Unfortunately, their campaign was interrupted when co-leader Metiria Turei, criticising Work and Income—the government body which administers social welfare—and in solidarity with people receiving benefits, revealed that she had committed benefit fraud as a single mother in the 1990s. Although she received some support for her stand, she also faced criticism, and she eventually stepped down as co-leader.

The National Party gained a majority of votes in that election, but under our mixed-member proportional (MMP) system the balance of power fell to New Zealand First, a small party headed by populist Winston Peters. In a controversial move, Peters decided to form a coalition with the centre-left

Labour Party and the Green Party, and 37-year-old Jacinda Ardern became our third female prime minister, declaring that her government would be 'focused, empathetic, and strong'. In January 2018, Ardern announced that she was pregnant, and later that year she made history when Neve, her daughter, joined her at the United Nations. Also, and perhaps most positively, there has been a resurgence of interest in our indigenous Māori cultures, and in te reo Māori (the Māori language) in particular, with many more adults learning it.

Internationally, there has been an increasing focus on love in politics, which I discuss in several of these pieces. This has come about partly in resistance to the fear and hatred that characterises modern politics; but it has also arisen in response to many people's growing recognition of our mutuality. For many of us, the last four years have made the need for loving politics that much easier to appreciate.

The world continues to change.

I will not attempt to list all of the people who have influenced my thinking on the Politics of Love. (There is plenty of evidence of this in the pieces themselves, as well as in the acknowledgements and bibliography at the end of this book.) It would be remiss of me, however, not to mention the ways in which experiences have informed the development of my ideas over the last four years.

Two things have been especially important, and have shaped the Politics of Love. First, I transitioned from a vegetarian diet to a vegan lifestyle. Like most people, I was brought up eating meat, but a number of years ago, affected by the suffering of animals, I adopted a vegetarian diet. In 2016,

I went vegan, motivated primarily by environmental concerns, and with the support of my then-girlfriend. This has been an intellectual journey as much as a lifestyle change, bringing me into contact with animal rights, environmentalist, and—most valuably—ecofeminist theory. These ideas have informed my understanding of politics.

Second, I recognised my Māori ancestry, through my maternal grandmother, and reconnected with my Kāi Tahu heritage. (Kāi Tahu, or Ngāi Tahu, is the largest iwi, or tribe, of Te Waipounamu, the South Island of New Zealand.) I had grown up believing I was only Pākehā (New Zealand European). In 2012, I began learning te reo Māori, and a little while later I started working as a research assistant at Te Kupenga Hauora Māori, the Department of Māori Health at The University of Auckland, looking at Kaupapa Māori (or Māori-centred) theory and research. The understanding I gained in those contexts influenced my thinking and—eventually—enabled me to reclaim my Kāi Tahu heritage. The influence of whakaaro Māori (Māori thinking) on the Politics of Love is significant.

It is appropriate that I mention my use of te reo Māori throughout this book. Although I often give the English meaning alongside the Māori in the text, sometimes I do not. Why is this? Well, sometimes, as I was writing, the context encouraged me to 'give way' to te reo, as my indigenous language; and when I considered translating it in the text, doing so seemed to diminish it. In many cases, you will be able to discern the meaning from the context; in most instances where the meaning is unclear, you will find the kupu in the glossary. If this intrudes on your reading, I hope you will forgive me and trust that I have good reasons for deferring to my indigenous language, even if those reasons are not immediately apparent to you.

Throughout this book, I discuss a number of criticisms of the Politics of Love. I want to address two prominent critiques here. The first, which many people make, is that the Politics of Love is 'too idealistic'. This criticism does not hold. In the messy world of politics, we need motivating ideals to keep us focused on what is important to us.

It is true that we will not solve all of the world's problems (we should be deeply suspicious of any theory that claims to be able to do this), but we must continually confront them. Albert Camus discusses this problem in his book *The Rebel*:

> Man can master, in himself, everything that should be mastered. He should rectify in creation everything that can be rectified. And after he has done so, children will still die unjustly even in a perfect society. Even by his greatest effort, man can only propose to diminish, arithmetically, the sufferings of the world. But the injustice and suffering of the world will remain and, no matter how limited they are, they will not cease to be an outrage.

Nonetheless, we must engage in the spirit of rebellion. As Camus insists, we should resist the conditions of our suffering—our own, and other people's—even as we know that those conditions will never be fully transcended.

A related concern is that the Politics of Love does not offer specific solutions to our problems. As I demonstrate with the pieces in this collection, however, love *does* suggest solutions, to a diverse range of issues. Much more importantly, it provides a framework with which solutions to our problems can be generated.

The second criticism I want to address here is that the Politics of Love is 'unrealistic'. This criticism is especially pernicious, and it takes several forms. One form that this argument takes is that people are not 'good enough', or loving enough, for the Politics of Love. We are, some people claim, too greedy, too selfish, too willing to put our own interests above those of others, to realise loving politics. I reject this cynical view of human nature. I believe one reason that some of us have become habitually selfish is because we teach each other that that's how people are. (We're repeatedly told that most people are self-serving— that ultimately, people only care about themselves. Is it really any wonder that some of us act that way?) I believe we are essentially good, and that when we show each other love, the best in all of us reveals itself.

Sometimes, we are prevented from loving not by other people, but by ourselves. One reason for this is that we know we are imperfect. We can be persuaded by the thought that, because we are not perfectly loving, we are unloving or incapable of love. I can recall times when I have said and done things which have been unloving. Who am I, then, to say 'love'? None of us comes close to loving perfectly. Although I believe that this understanding should move us toward humility, I do not think that it should prevent anyone from trying to make the world a better place. (If all of us took that excuse, who would do the work of love?)

If you are reading this thinking, 'I cannot love, because there are times when I have not been loving,' I would like to say to you: I know that thought well, and I know the pain it brings with it. I have found wisdom in the words of Thích Nhất Hạnh, who writes:

> What is important is to reconcile within your own heart and mind. If reconciliation is done within, that is enough. Because the effect of that reconciliation will be felt everywhere later on. . . . Reconciliation means to work it out within yourself so that peace can be restored. Reconcile with yourself for the sake of the world, for the sake of all living beings. Your peace and serenity are crucial for all of us.

When we stand up for love—as imperfect as we all know we are—we teach each other that it is okay to do so. It is vitally important that we do this, because love needs *all* of us feeling, thinking, and acting. It is true that there is risk in doing this. As James Baldwin writes, 'To act is to be committed, and to be committed is to be in danger.' Still, if we believe in love, we must be willing to affirm that although none of us will ever be 'perfect', we are good enough, and that, although there is danger in doing so, we are ready to love.

Another form this argument takes is that if we enact loving values, such as *trust*, we will be taken advantage of by 'bad', or unscrupulous, people. I believe we inhabit the world that we create. When we give expression to loving values, we encourage other people to do the same; by doing so, we will create a community in which everyone feels confident to love. *He aroha whakatō, he aroha puta mai.* (If love is sown, then love will grow.)

Still other people contend that we should set 'realistic' goals, and lower our expectations. They point out that incremental change is more achievable; and so, they argue, we should focus on that, rather than radical movement. This will at least get us somewhere, and it will prevent us from being disappointed when our Utopian schemes fail to bring the change we were hoping for. Anyway, they say, isn't it more honest to be pessimistic, considering the facts? However, in her book *Psychology for a Better World: Strategies to Inspire Sustainability*, Niki Harré affirms the importance of positive narratives. For example, she explains that focusing on the negative consequences of inaction discourages positive behaviours, because it makes us feel doomed; whereas focusing on what we *can* do, and the positive things that people like us are *already* doing, encourages us to do what we can, because it gives promise to our actions. If we want to see positive change, we must talk in terms of possibility.

I also want to address a widespread misconception about love—which is that it requires self-sacrifice. Although it is true that love sometimes involves sacrifice, it is only in extreme circumstances that it asks us to sacrifice *ourselves*. As I argue in these pieces, self-love (which is not to be confused with selfishness, nor with narrow self-interest) is essential. Some people think that politics is primarily about mediating self-interest, and that it is right for all individuals to try to get 'the best deal' for themselves with minimal regard for others—and only realistic to expect them to. The idea that ethics, or morality, *only* involves sacrifice is widespread. Those who have learnt to think about politics in this way—as a means of managing various people's competing interests—may view the Politics of Love with suspicion, believing that it will not benefit them, and might even leave them worse off. But the suggestion that loving politics does not benefit those who work for it is false: all of us stand to gain from living in a more nurturing world. However, to focus exclusively on how politics benefits you individually is at odds with the project of loving politics. The Politics of Love urges us to extend our circle of concern beyond ourselves—to other people, to non-human animals, and to the natural environment.

As I have mentioned, the Politics of Love is a values-based politics. I explore numerous values throughout the pieces in this collection, but I would like to highlight one here, and that is *courage*. I believe that *courage* is especially important to the realisation of loving politics, and that it is particularly needed now. It takes courage to stand up for what we believe. The fear of being ridiculed sometimes stops us from doing the right thing, and the worry that we will be dismissed prevents many people from speaking of love. Unfortunately, a lot of people still do not take loving politics seriously. If we really believe that the Politics of Love is what our world needs, we must stand up for it. We must affirm its importance, with words and with actions, against our worries and against our fears. Every time you use the word 'love' to advocate for a better world, you add to its power. As more of us use it, it will become less ridiculous and less easily dismissed. Soon, its importance will be as clear to everyone else as it is to us.

In sharing these pieces, my hope is that those who are already working for a better world will unite around the Politics of Love, recognising its potential to realise our common goal, and that more and more people will join in the difficult and rewarding work of love.

I hope you will, too.

The Politics of Love

Max Harris and Philip McKibbin

This article originally appeared on The Aotearoa Project in May 2015.

Around the world, progressive-minded people are struggling to articulate an end-goal for politics. The Right, in most places, remains committed to the tight logic of neoliberalism (and its ideals of private property, liberty, and efficiency). The Left, meanwhile, has failed to respond. There are some who still have faith in a Marxist vision of the total collapse of capitalism; others in the radical tradition hold onto religious prophecies. But for the rest of us, the direction our political journey should take has become unclear. We do not know where we are going. At the same time, there is a growing disdain of politics generally, especially amongst young people. Politicians don't look like us, they don't behave like we do, and their ideas don't connect to our needs. There is deep doubt, in other words, about whether politics is the right vehicle for collective struggle—even if we could settle on the destination of our journey.

And when we look to the work of academics and writers, we see end-goals and ideals that fail to inspire confidence. The grand ideas of political philosophy are often rarefied. Human dignity, for example, is an attractive concept, but it requires considerable intellectual work to connect it to the realities of everyday life. And thinktanks are invariably too close to the political sphere to contribute anything imaginative or truly original.

We like to think we are exceptional in Aotearoa New Zealand, but the politics of this country is not exempt from these trends. The Left has not voiced a shared vision for a better society—other than referring, in passing, to values like 'decency' and 'fairness'. And there is alienation from politics here, too: around one million people stayed at home on Election Day in 2014, a lot of them younger people. The proliferation of political parties on the Left suggests the need for a more unified narrative. And here, as elsewhere, writers and universities—the engines of ideas in our society—have failed to produce that narrative to fill the gap in public debate.

It would be a mistake to think, though, that we, as New Zealanders, are incapable of addressing these problems. We have a history of progressive politics that has positively influenced the trajectory of world history. The narratives we tell our children—involving women's suffrage, indigenous rights, our anti-nuclear stance, and homosexual law reform—provide examples not only to ourselves, but for people everywhere.

So what is to be done? We think the answer lies, at least partially, in articulating a values-based politics. More specifically, we think the answer can be found in the values of everyday life. Some of these values, like kindness, have been relegated to the private domain—for what is, in our view, no good reason. Perhaps it is thought that these values are too virtuous to be respected consistently and in public by our politicians. Whatever the case, we believe these are values that we can rally around. Bringing politics closer to our lived values will ensure we are less alienated from politicians; it may also help to humanise the ideas that are developed by political philosophers and thinktanks.

In this article, we sketch a *politics of love*, in the spirit of finding a politics grounded in everyday values. Love itself might be understood as a value, but we think it can also be understood as a way of determining what is valuable. We view it as underlying other everyday values that could be part of a new political vision.

We are not the first people to suggest that love might helpfully inform politics. In her book *All About Love*, bell hooks writes, 'All the great social movements for freedom and justice in our society have promoted a love ethic. . . . Were a love ethic informing all public policy in cities and towns, individuals would come together and map out programmes that would affect the good of everyone. . . .' Jimmy Carter, the spiritually minded and ethically grounded US president, talked of the need for a 'government filled with love'. And Vaclav Havel, the musician and playwright and Czech statesman, who led the fight to free his country from Soviet rule, said that a government must 'radiate love'. This is not an exhaustive list of references to love in politics, either. Martin

Luther King, Jr. focused on the idea in his speeches, Hone Harawira encouraged the New Zealand government to pass a bill providing free school lunches as a 'show of love', and many others (including the group Heart Politics in Aotearoa New Zealand) have invoked love in similar ways.

What did these thinkers, writers, activists, and politicians mean by 'love', and how might we understand the concept? bell hooks chooses to understand love as 'the will to extend one's self for the purpose of nurturing one's own or another's spiritual growth'. Love, for us, is a sentiment of enduring warmth toward a person or people, which shows a deep concern for them. It can be expressed in different ways—for example, through words or in actions. It is closely connected to kindness, generosity, and commitment. The Māori concept of *aroha*, which is best understood in its cultural context, enriches our understanding of love by articulating something a little wider, a little deeper. In his book *Tikanga Whakaaro*, Cleve Barlow writes that aroha is a creative force which emanates from the gods.

He aha te aroha? Ko te aroha he tikanga whakaaro nui; ka aroha tētahi tangata ki tētahi tangata, ki tōna iwi, whenua hoki, ki ngā kīrehe, ki ngā manu, ki ngā ika, ki ngā mea katoa e tupu ake ana i te whenua. Ka aroha te tangata ki tētahi atu, ahakoa he aha tōna āhua i roto i ōna pikitanga ake, i roto anō i ōna heketanga iho, i roto i ōna hari, i roto i ōna pōuri, i roto i āna mahi pai me āna mahi hē.

(What is aroha? Aroha in a person is an all-encompassing quality of goodness, expressed by love for people, land, birds and animals, fish, and all living things. A person who has aroha for another expresses genuine concern toward them and acts with their welfare in mind, no matter what their state of health or wealth.)

Barlow emphasises the actively inclusive quality of love:

Ko te tangata e mea ana he aroha tōna, ka taea e ia te kite, te atawhai te iwi whānui ahakoa iti, ahakoa rahi.

(A person who claims to possess the gift of aroha demonstrates this love by sharing it with all people and without discrimination.)

We think that these understandings can inform our thinking and guide us in love. We would encourage everyone to reflect further on how love can be understood and interpreted, so that together we can work for the good of all people. *Aroha mai, aroha atu.*

If these understandings tell us something about what love *is*, what might a politics of love look like? We think love encourages us all to care about politics. If love involves a concern for people, then a politics of love will move this world to a better place for everyone. We can, of course, attempt to make our world a better place in lots of ways: by building character, for example, or by improving our relationships. But when we reflect on the many ways in which politics affects our well-being, it becomes clear that to love—to express a sentiment of enduring warmth toward a person or people—is, in part, to care about politics. This point can be brought out negatively: if we fail to resist racism or sexism, issues that are largely political, we cannot be said to be loving, we cannot be said to care about people. If we are committed to changing the structure of our society, politics must be part of the project; and if politics is going to do the work of love, it will be because we as individuals care enough to ensure that it does.

In such a politics, love would be woven through all of our policy. Embracing a politics of love would change how we justify policy, as well as how we talk about it. For example, welfare and benefits might be understood not in terms of encouraging re-entry into the work force (an economic justification), but rather as an expression of commitment toward certain individuals and groups in society that require support. And a politics of love would rule out 'beneficiary-bashing' language, which does not, and cannot, evince love for those who receive benefits. As another example, refugee policy might be reconceived as a way of showing warmth to persecuted individuals, in the same way that hospitality can be seen as an expression of love for outsiders. The politics of love could change how policy is delivered, and how the state is seen by those affected by policy.

Love could also prompt substantive rethinking in certain areas. Guided by love, policy-makers may choose to abandon certain policies, and to pursue others more vigorously. This will have to be debated, and we do not want to pre-empt the outcome of those debates here. But to illustrate our point, a politics of love might spark a renewed focus on rehabilitation in prisons, as an expression of the principle that warmth should be shown to all individuals, even those who have made mistakes, and of our understanding that individuals are never wholly responsible for their situations. A politics of love might also lead to the apportioning of more funding to community activities and support—such as counselling helplines and sports clubs—since these institutions help to build bonds of love among those who share a community. The aim, in this new politics, would be to achieve the preconditions of love within a community, as well as to express love itself.

Love requires that we recognise the importance of *all* people, and a politics of love would encourage us to ensure that this recognition informs every political decision that we make: in deciding whether to vote, and who to vote for; in running for office, or deciding whether to support those who are; in helping to make policy, or deciding how to respond to it. . . . We should also be aware that a lot of actions that do not seem political have a political dimension. Engaging in politics is a broader enterprise than we might think: who we are friends with, how we talk to others, how we operate in the so-called 'private domain' of the home—all of this is political, as feminists have long maintained. A politics of love would have love run through all of these decisions and interactions. It could, then, be an ethical framework as well as a political approach.

Also integral to a politics of love is collectivity. A love ethic, in bell hooks's terms, brings people together and reminds us of the value of relationships and collective endeavour. In

Aotearoa New Zealand, te ao Māori gives us special insight into collectivity and how it might be understood: with its emphasis on collective well-being, it encourages us all to adopt a progressive understanding of politics, focused on enhancing the well-being of us all. We, collectively, are responsible for the world we share, and a focus on the strengths of collectives might help us make political decisions that better balance the needs of individuals, and that respond appropriately to the natural world on which we are so dependent.

It is likely that disagreements will arise as to how such an abstract term like 'love' is to be interpreted for, and applied to, politics. But the importance of love is something we should all be able to agree on. Are we advocating a politics of unconditional love, a politics where love can never be withdrawn? To this question, our answer is an unwavering 'yes'. We believe the state owes love to all of its citizens by virtue of our being people, and by virtue of the relationship between the state and its people. The state may express love in stronger or weaker ways, but love itself must never be abandoned, and we should not be drawn into debates about whether love might be withheld, or withdrawn, from some individuals (such as prisoners). Others may say, as a further objection, that love is too soft—too airy-fairy, too waffly—for the hard discussions that need to be had in politics. We reject this claim, too. It is true that politics is not easy, and that (re-)introducing love into the political arena will not resolve or dissolve all disputes. But it is precisely because politics is messy and difficult that we need motivating ideals—like love—that can keep us focused on what matters in potentially divisive debates.

One of the special things about values is that they are able to inform complex decision-making processes while maintaining their integrity, or purity, as values. In contrast to more prescriptive approaches, values can inspire action without compromising their capacity to provide us with different solutions in different situations. And there are numerous values that we encounter in everyday life that could also be translated into politics. These include (but are by no means limited to) compassion, responsibility, forgiveness, and honesty. We suggest that these can be understood in relation to, and interpreted through, love, but as these are complex issues, we will have to explore these values elsewhere.

The politics of love that we have sketched demonstrates that everyday values can provide a wellspring of resources for a new vision of politics. This is a view of politics that is more grounded, and at the same time more imaginative, than other narratives circulating today. We are suggesting that the direction our politics should take need not be based on some theory produced through detached reflection, or taken from some distant political movement. Maybe we have been living with it all along. Maybe it has been all around us, waiting. Maybe in politics as in life—to end with the words of a song—all you need is love.

The authors wish to thank Simon Waigth and Lana Doyle for their helpful comments on a draft of this article.

2

Marriage, Equality, and Love

Earlier this month [June 2015], Nick Jensen published an article in the *Canberra CityNews*, in which he declares that he and his wife Sarah have decided to divorce if Australia allows same sex couples to marry. His article has generated a lot of controversy—but what interests me more are comments he made after the article was published, about the relationship between marriage and love.

It isn't my intention to address all of Jensen's arguments here. Most of what he says only makes sense if you accept the existence of the Christians' god, which I am unable to do. If you're interested, you can read his article.[2]

You might ask, Why should I care? If fearful people want to fracture their lives for a foolish cause, why should *we* care? It isn't as if their threat to divorce is going to change anyone's mind, is it?

Unfortunately, such actions *do* have consequences. We cannot not care. The fact is, there are still many people who oppose, or are ambivalent about, marriage equality. Some of these people will be receptive to such political action. The

2   http://citynews.com.au/2015/gay-law-change-may-force-us-to-divorce/

harms associated with marriage inequality are significant—and we must resist all of them. For gay people, these include the obvious constraints on choice, as well as the harms that come from knowing society values your self and happiness less than other people's. It also has consequences that affect us all: some of these connect to the notion that difference is unacceptable, and others to the idea that inequality *is* acceptable. Nick Jensen's announcement will influence people's thinking, which is why we must resist it: in democracies, it's the people who (supposedly) determine policy, and inequality has serious implications for well-being.

The Jensens' decision is especially interesting, as it's an example of private, or personal, action that is having political consequences. Nick Jensen has, it would seem, gone out of his way to attract attention to his cause. However, I would argue that even if he and Sarah had only shared their reasons with their close friends and family, their actions would still be political, and the consequences would still be significant. They would be using their decision to divorce as an argument to influence other people; and the consequences, were that decision to go unanswered, would be unnecessary harm to people other than themselves. The personal is political, and each of us has a responsibility to act in ways that enhance, rather than diminish, well-being—our own and other people's.

The issue of marriage equality—like gay rights generally—is an issue of love. Max Harris and I recently sketched a 'politics of love', in which we argue for a love-infused, values-based politics. I think love can inform all of our political decisions, but it gives us especially clear guidance on gay marriage, as marriage and equality are issues that relate to love in special ways.

Most people would agree that marriage has a lot to do with love. But in commenting on his article, Jensen was emphatic in saying that marriage shouldn't be understood as being primarily about love. Instead, he suggested, it has more to do with raising children.[3]

This point needs to be addressed, as it is a significant one. It's logically inconsistent to hold that, because they cannot have biological children together, gay people shouldn't be allowed to marry *if we do not also hold* that heterosexual couples who cannot conceive shouldn't be allowed to marry. If we were to decide to prevent people who are incapable of having children together from marrying, we would have to stop old couples who love each other but who can no longer have children from marrying. We might also test prospective marriage partners to see whether or not they are able to conceive, and if they aren't, refuse to grant them marriage licences. These suggestions are, of course, atrocious—and that's the point. Logical consistency requires us to accept that preventing gay couples from marrying because they cannot have biological children together is equally as atrocious.

Marriage has more to do with love than with raising children. And I would suggest that to support gay marriage is the loving thing to do, whereas to resist it is unloving. If marriage is a celebration of love, involving respect, responsibility, and commitment, then it seems unreasonable

3 http://www.stuff.co.nz/life-style/love-sex/69287363/couple-vow-to-divorce-if-australia-legalises-samesex-marriage

to me to prevent consenting adults from engaging in it. Whether the partners are gay or straight is irrelevant, as it doesn't affect their ability to choose, or indicate how loving the marriage will be.

I have to admit: I'm not a huge fan of marriage. I believe we can nurture lasting relationships that involve respect, responsibility, and commitment without marrying. (I also have specific concerns about marriage, which I may explore in another article.) But these views don't affect my stance on gay marriage, because marriage equality isn't about marriage so much as it's about equality. I think love requires us to respect equality. I understand love as involving a concern for people; and a concern for people is, necessarily, a concern for *all* people. The idea of moral equality is integral to this, because without it, our supposed 'concern for people' is reduced to a concern for *some* people: for family, for friends, for people who are 'like' us, or who aren't 'unlike' us. Love is for *all* people.

Although they've got a lot wrong, the conservatives have got at least one thing right in debates about gay marriage— something which we progressives have been reluctant to acknowledge—and that is that marriage equality will have profound implications for our understanding of relationships. We've been reluctant to acknowledge this because doing so risked lending legitimacy to conservatives' more fanciful claims (that gay marriage will lead to sex with ducks, for example) as well as their more harmful assertions (such as that gay marriage will lead to adults marrying children). But as marriage equality becomes a reality in more places, I think more and more people will question their basic assumptions, re-evaluating much that has been accepted uncritically—including the value of marriage itself.

In fact, Nick Jensen's stunt has encouraged me to re-examine one of my assumptions. In commenting on his article, he said, 'Once you say that marriage is detached from children, [that it's] just about love, then when three people come to the state and say 'well we're all in love', then the state has no grounds . . . to say why they can't get married.' Reflecting on this, I have had to concede that he has a point, although it has led me even further from his conclusions. If three adults love each other and want to get married, I honestly can't see why they should be prevented from making such a commitment to one another. I imagine a three-person marriage would be less practical in certain respects than a two-person one. But I don't think this is a strong enough consideration to prevent consenting adults from exercising their capacity to choose.

I suspect, and hope, that one of the legacies of marriage equality will be a move away from rigidly defined, exclusive unions, toward more inclusive relationships that give expression to the Ancient Greek concept of *agape*, or universal love. Such relationships would reflect a concern for all people. (Incidentally, Martin Luther King, Jr. identifies *agape*, the love for all people, as 'the love of God operating in the human heart'.) In other words, marriage equality could help to move all of us *away from* marriage, toward more loving relationships.

Marriage equality gives all of us an opportunity to reflect on love and its importance not only in private life, but in public life as well. Some people have tried to frame gay marriage as a religious issue, but we needn't understand it as such. We should all be willing to affirm that, whether there's a god or not, we as people are capable of love. Supporting marriage equality is one way that we can do this.

Note: Same-sex marriage was legalised by the Australian parliament in December 2017. The Jensens have yet to announce their divorce.

3

Hijacked Emotions

Fighting Terrorism with Love

This article originally appeared on *openDemocracy*'s *Transformation* in December 2015.

In the aftermath of the terrorist attacks at and around the Bataclan theatre in Paris last month, amid all the talk of war and destruction, some people could be heard calling for love. But what would a loving response to terrorism be?

I understand love as a concern for all people, which has well-being as its first focus. It is, importantly, opposed to what Martin Luther King, Jr. describes as 'the barbaric consequences of any tribal-centered, national-centered, or racial-centered ethic'—of which terrorism and its causes (many of which the West is responsible for) provide us with numerous examples.

Terrorists do not believe in love. They are not trying to realise a world in which all people matter. If they were, they would quickly see that the hate they generate works against, rather than for, this ideal. Their aims are much narrower, as their actions suggest: those who have faith in people do not murder them. In responding to terrorism, we must assume responsibility for this serious problem, and disarm those who exacerbate it.

In her book *All About Love*, bell hooks emphasises will and work. These two concepts are especially useful, as they can help us to translate 'love' into political practice. According to hooks, will is more than mere intention: it requires endurance and it generates action. In saying that love involves work, she teaches that it requires effort.

Another important element of love, which is often overlooked, is intellectual engagement. Love is typically understood in emotional terms; but to conceive of love *only* in emotional terms would be a mistake. If we are to love, it is not enough to feel; we must also think.

Terrorists try to hijack our emotions; for this reason, we should be wary of allowing our emotions to dictate the ways in which we respond to terrorism. Terrorists want us to feel shock, outrage, insecurity—*terror*. The manipulation of our emotions is integral to their strategy. Intellectual engagement can support us in responding reasonably to terrorism.

It is worth reiterating that the aim of terrorism is to terrorise: terrorists want us to feel fear. They know that this is an effective way to engage our attention; and they believe, with good reason, that by assaulting our emotions, they can provoke us into responding in hateful ways—in ways, that is, that 'justify' violent action, not only to other people, but to themselves.

In May, Max Harris and I published an article entitled 'The Politics of Love', in which we argued for a values-based politics. I think that the Politics of Love, which we sketched, can help us to think clearly about how we should respond to terrorism.

So, what would a loving response to terrorism involve?

It would be proactive, rather than reactive: it would see us responding to the causes of terrorism, rather than concerning ourselves disproportionately with terrorist actions. We should be very concerned about talk of violence and war—of, that is to say, *all* forms of terrorism. It is a painful fact (albeit one that many of us experience only as discomfort) that 'legitimate' states enact much more violence worldwide than terror groups do.

I would suggest that the most loving and effective approach governments could take to defuse international terrorism would be to immediately adopt peaceful processes in their dealings with other peoples. As well as demonstrating our concern for all people and our opposition to all forms of terrorism, this strategy would deprive terror groups of one of the most compelling justifications for the violence they perpetrate.

A loving response to terrorism would involve recognising our interrelatedness, and taking seriously the legitimate concerns of all peoples and all people—including those communities whose members are vulnerable to radicalisation, and even individuals who commit acts of terrorism.

Importantly, it would see us looking beyond terrorist acts to the causes of terrorism: namely, the ongoing exploitation of powerless countries by the West and its allies. (This exploitation does not excuse terrorist action, but it does explain it; and it is only when we properly understand a problem that we can think clearly about solving it.) Undertaking this examination would lead to a focus on foreign development that prioritises both human rights and relative autonomy, nurturing love between people and peoples. It would also see wealthy nations providing sanctuary to refugees fleeing unloving situations.

A loving response to terrorism would necessarily be part of a wider re-imagining of politics, and so would have broad implications. It would challenge capitalism and its institutions, by, for example, requiring the reconfiguration of our profit-driven media, which has been so effectively exploited by terrorists. They understand that sensationalism sells; that the more outrageous their actions, the more attention they will receive. Loving media models, by contrast, prioritise critical analysis and creative discussion aimed at promoting understanding and peaceful resolutions.

When we commit to love, we will undoubtedly encounter criticism from those who, echoing President François Hollande's vow to 'destroy' Daesh, would have us respond to terrorism with violence. When this happens, we would do well to remember Abraham Lincoln's response during the American Civil War to someone who accused him of taking too conciliatory an approach in dealing with the South. 'Madam,' he said, 'do I not destroy my enemies when I make them my friends?'

Love requires us to think of terrorists as people. It encourages us to understand that their actions, however hateful, come from a place of grievance. It asks us to believe that their pain, and the pain that so many other people in so many places around the world are feeling in this time of terror, is not insurmountable—that, collectively, we are able to overcome it.

4

For the Love of Animals

This article originally appeared in the NZ Vegetarian Society's magazine, *Vegetarian Living NZ*, in
January 2016.

All around the world, people are becoming more aware of
the suffering of animals and are beginning to think critically
about our treatment of them. Many of us are trying to eat
ethically, and more and more people are transitioning to
vegetarianism and veganism.

At the same time, we are realising that love must play a role
in politics. Most recently, this has been seen in the realisation
of marriage equality in the United States of America, and in
the inspiring stances Canadian Prime Minister Justin Trudeau
has taken, especially with respect to Canada's indigenous
peoples and refugees.

It is timely to ask, What role should the interests of
animals play in our politics?

In May last year, Max Harris and I published an article
called 'The Politics of Love', in which we argued for a values-
based politics infused with love. We believe that love has a

central role to play in our politics. I think that the theory we sketched can accommodate a concern for animal welfare, and guide us as we work to promote the interests of animals.

There are many reasons for caring about animals. The appalling conditions in which animals are 'farmed'—the fact that globally, nearly fifty billion animals spend their entire lives in tiny confinement systems, unable to experience sunshine, fresh air, exercise, or even the ability to turn around—is a strong motivation for many of us to change our lifestyles. We all feel that there is something objectionable about unnecessary suffering, and when we begin to appreciate the scale of suffering that factory 'farming' entails, and discover that there are viable alternatives to this, we realise that the case for change is compelling.

It is also important that we recognise the harmful effects the meat and dairy industries have on the environment, and the benefits associated with reducing the volume of animal products that we collectively consume. In 2010, the United Nations advocated a global shift toward meat- and dairy-free diets, reporting that diets high in meat and dairy are unsustainable for the environment. And as we know, the health of the planet affects animals as well as people.

There are self-interested reasons for changing our behaviour, too. In his book *Eating Animals*, Jonathan Safran Foer notes that vegetarian diets are suitable for all individuals at all stages of the lifecycle; that they are typically lower in saturated fat and cholesterol and higher in other important nutrients; and that they are often associated with health advantages, including lower risk of heart disease, and lower overall cancer rates. He writes:

> I talked to several leading American nutritionists about this—taking both adults and children as the subjects of my questions—and heard the same thing again and again: vegetarianism is at least as healthy as a diet that includes meat.

And as millions of people worldwide are proving, vegan diets can be exceptionally healthy, too.

What, then, does love have to do with animals?

In his little book *How to Love*, Zen Master Thích Nhất Hạnh emphasises the connection between body and mind. In teaching us how to nourish our love, he writes, 'If we eat with moderation, eating only the foods we need and eating the foods that help our bodies to be strong and healthy, then we're showing love and respect for our bodies and for the Earth.' Eating in a respectful way can serve as the basis for our respect of other people, and for the planet.

We know that love concerns itself with people, but it should also concern itself with animals. I follow Martin Luther King, Jr. and others in holding love to be a concern for *all* people. I think about Minnie, the cat who lives with my father's family. I love Minnie, and I feel that, because we have similar temperaments, we understand each other. She is sometimes grumpy, which I suspect is because I call her Minnie Mouse! And we consider her and Galli, her frenemy, to be family members. I know that many people feel similarly about their pets. If we can extend our concern for people beyond those we are already close to—such as our family, our friends—can we not also extend our concern for animals in a similar way, recognising the importance not only of the animals we have befriended, but of all animals, as animals, and because they have interests? I believe that we can.

Even if you do not have pets or are not especially fond of animals, you will know from the interactions you have had with them that they have interests, and that, like us, they suffer when mistreated. This should make you concerned.

That the animals we use for food suffer is generally well-known, even if the particulars of their suffering are not. As I have written elsewhere, intellectual engagement is integral to love, and each of us has a responsibility to educate ourselves about harmful practices. If you would like to learn more about 'farming' practices, I would encourage you to visit Compassion in World Farming's website at www.ciwf.com.

So, what would loving political action look like with respect to animals?

The most immediate and effective action we can take as individuals with respect to the interests of animals is to reduce our consumption of animal products, and a loving politics would acknowledge the importance of such action.

In our original article, Max Harris and I wrote:

We should . . . be aware that a lot of actions that do not seem political have a political dimension. Engaging in politics is a broader enterprise than we might think: who we are friends with, how we talk to others, how we operate in the so-called 'private domain' of the home—all of this is political, as feminists have long maintained. A politics of love would have love run through all of these decisions and interactions.

Eating ethically is an excellent example of everyday political action. As well as directly impacting loving political goals (think of the suffering that we avoid), it reduces demand for harmful practices and institutions, and thereby encourages alternative industries that are less harmful to animals and the planet. It sets an example for other people, and so has the potential to influence opinions in the way that, say, standing up to sexism does. And it opens opportunities for dialogue, not only about the huge difference we can make with our lifestyle choices, but about the importance of animal interests and welfare. All of this can, and should, be understood as political.

The Politics of Love would see all of us becoming vegetarians and, ideally, vegans. Although making such lifestyle changes can be difficult to begin with, vegetarians and vegans will tell you that there is much fulfilment to be gained in knowing that we are acting lovingly and choosing not to contribute to the suffering of animals.

There is also a role for more 'traditional' forms of political action. As individuals, we can work to achieve higher animal welfare standards by supporting the campaigns of animal welfare organisations, by lobbying for better legislation to protect animals, and by choosing to vote for political parties that endorse high standards of animal welfare (to offer only a few examples). Indeed, it is political engagement of this nature that has led to improvements in animal welfare legislation and regulations: for instance, Aotearoa New Zealand's recent bans on sow stalls and cosmetic testing on animals. Such outcomes suggest that, as individuals, we are able to contribute positively to meaningful change for animals.

It is important to remember that our well-being, the welfare of animals, and the health of the planet that we all share are intimately connected. Any politics that takes love, or even people, as its focus would perpetuate as many problems as it fixed if it failed to attend critically to our use (and abuse) of animals. We should actively concern ourselves with these issues.

The Politics of Love, as well as being a politics of people, is a politics that recognises animal interests and concerns itself with them. All of us must act to make our world more loving.

I wish to thank Danielle Duffield for her helpful comments on a draft of this article.

5

It Is Time to Imagine Our Entire Politics in Loving Terms

This article originally appeared in the *Guardian* in June 2017.

Something important is missing from politics. Around the world we see division, and in some areas hate is gaining ground. Much of the progress that has been made toward unity is being undone, and those of us who long for a more caring world find ourselves questioning whether we will achieve it.

We might ask, 'Why can't love, which is so central to our personal relationships, also guide our political relationships?' The Politics of Love strives to answer that question.

Max Harris and I first sketched the Politics of Love in 2015. It is a values-based politics, which affirms the importance of people, and extends beyond us to non-human animals and the environment. Central to the Politics of Love are loving values, such as *compassion* and *commitment*, which can guide action and inform policy.

The idea that love might influence politics is not new. It has precedents in the everyday acts of love we show to one another, as well as in the feminist, civil rights, and LGBTQI movements. As African American thinker bell hooks writes in her book *All About Love*, 'All the great social movements for freedom and justice in our society have promoted a love ethic.'

I think it is time to imagine our entire politics in loving terms.

What do I mean by love? Love can be understood as a value, but it is more than a value: it determines and balances other loving values—like *responsibility*, *understanding*, and *fairness*. Love is a way of relating: to ourselves, and to the world around us. And, as Martin Luther King, Jr. teaches in his sermon 'On Being a Good Neighbor', it is universal: love is for everyone. I have come to think of love as much more than 'a warm feeling': it is a combination of care, concern, and commitment.

Most of us already think that love is important. The Politics of Love insists that we act. It engages us individually and collectively, in our everyday lives as well as in policy. And it is open: it asks, and requires, all of us to contribute to its development. But it is not so open that 'anything goes': it is anti-racist, anti-sexist, and against all forms of exploitation. As bell hooks writes in *Feminism Is for Everybody*, 'there can be no love when there is domination'.

You probably already agree that we should try to love in our day-to-day interactions, but what might loving policy look like?

In education, the Politics of Love might see us promoting loving values. One way we could do this in settler-colonial societies is by teaching young people our indigenous languages. In Aotearoa New Zealand, where I am from, we could make te reo Māori (the Māori language) compulsory in schools. As an adult learner of te reo Māori, I have seen how it can bring people together and extend our understanding. Importantly, teaching our indigenous languages in schools could support decolonising efforts.

In health, the Politics of Love, with its values of *care, concern*, and *moral equality*, would see us focusing on disadvantage. We might aim to create a 'loving system', which, rather than shunting people from service to service, would 'wrap around' people, nurturing them throughout their lives. This would require *creativity* and *collaboration*—in its development, and its implementation.

Also, I would like to see a radical reimagining of justice. What if, instead of thinking of justice in terms of retribution or revenge, we understood the ends of justice as the alleviation of suffering and the promotion of human dignity? In dealing with crime, we might seek to understand the people who have committed offences and work to address the causes of their offending, as well as caring for the victims of crime. Legal resolutions would be compassionate, inclusive, and restorative.

And love could guide us in international affairs. In my article 'Hijacked Emotions: Fighting Terrorism with Love', I argued that loving politics can address global terrorism. Eventually, it might also see us opening our borders.

Significantly, the Politics of Love requires us to re-think who and what politics concerns. Just as it suggests that we should take climate change seriously, in part as an expression of love to future generations, it requires that we show love to non-human animals, as sentient beings with interests.

The Politics of Love is not without its critics. It has been said that love is too weak a concept for politics. Max Harris and I anticipated this objection in our original article:

> It is true that politics is not easy, and that (re-) introducing love into the political arena will not resolve or dissolve all disputes. But it is precisely because politics is messy and difficult that we need motivating ideals—like love—that can keep us focused on what matters in potentially divisive debates.

Another criticism is that the word 'love' is too vague to give us any real guidance, that it can mean anything we want it to. 'Love' cannot mean all that it is currently used to mean, at least not in politics. Love is not exclusive (in the way that romantic love is generally thought to be). Nor is it only emotional: we must resist ways of understanding love that devalue intellectual engagement, as the failure to think, and to think clearly, is a major cause of many of the world's problems.

So, what must we do? The first requirement of the Politics of Love is that we care: about each other, and about politics. And we must work together, for the benefit of everyone. Values that could guide this are *mutuality*, *respect*, and *trust*. But we should also recognise the importance of individuals standing up—alone, if necessary—for what is right, and working in good faith to make our world a better place, especially when it seems that not enough people are.

The Politics of Love depends on us to realise it. We must resist those forces that would divide us, and strive—individually and collectively—to create a more caring world.

6

The Thin Line between Dickishness and Casual Racism

This article originally appeared on The Spinoff in July 2017.

I keep thinking about the wink the bartender gave me.

I didn't know then that he had just insulted my friends; I didn't even know most of them then. So I smiled, and did my awkward best to get on with the whakawhanaungatanga, greeting and welcoming as many of the newcomers as I could, while my hoa ako did the same.

I help to organise a reo Māori conversation group called Kapa Kōrero. We get together about once a month at different bars in Auckland to practice speaking te reo Māori and to enjoy each other's company. Almost all of us are second-language speakers, and most of us are still learning. One of our aims is to normalise te reo Māori in public spaces: to speak so it is heard.

We had been to this bar before, numerous times. We hadn't had problems—at least, not until recently. There had been the suggestion, made as I booked our table, that some of us would 'just drink water'. It's true: every now and then, one or two of us will drink water while sitting with our larger group. But most of us buy drinks, some of us buy more than one, and we often order snacks as well. I think the business has done pretty well out of us.

On this particular night, several of our group were stopped as they entered. They were told that they had to buy drinks then and there. They felt pressured into making a purchase, and did so. When one of our members approached the bar staff later that night, she was told, 'Well, when you see someone walk in and you have a feeling they're not gonna buy anything. . . .'

We were a darker, younger group that night; and it was a darker, younger subset of our members who were targeted. I believe they were targeted because they are Māori, and because they were part of our reo Māori group—which is to say, I believe it was racism.

Joanne McNaughton is one of Kapa Kōrero's founders. When she and I heard what had happened to our friends, we were angry. Jo and I had a kōrero about what to do—a conversation we continued over Messenger the next day.

A few days later, we sent a letter to the manager, explaining what had happened:

> We are ashamed of the way our members were treated. We want you to understand that when you treat one of us this way, although it is that person who is hurt

most by the treatment, all of us are affected: whether we are Māori or Pākehā, whether our skin is darker or lighter, whether we joined Kapa Kōrero two years ago or two minutes ago. When one of our members is emotionally assaulted, we worry for their well-being. No one should be publicly humiliated because of their ethnicity.

We wrote that we also worry for our reo: there are too few learners of te reo Māori, and the language needs all of them. Most of those who were targeted that night were newcomers to our group—and I know from experience how daunting it can be to attend a full-immersion hui for the first time.

While we were writing our letter, I spoke with one of my Pākehā friends about what had happened. He questioned whether it qualified as racism. It was 'dickish', he said, and they should definitely be called out on it, but was it racism? How could we prove it?

This is an important question. How *do* we know it was racism? The thing about racism is that it's often hard to tell it apart from 'dickishness'. Just as most racists don't run around yelling, 'I'm racist!', racism doesn't usually announce itself. The fact that racism is insidious (as Taika Waititi recently pointed out) makes it all the more necessary to call it out when it happens. We can only go by what we witnessed, what we were told, and what we have learnt. I can't imagine a group of Pākehā being treated that way.

I think about the bartender. We were greeting the newcomers and pulling together some seats; he had appeared to watch—to help, perhaps. When I looked up at him, he winked at me.

I look Pākehā—my skin is white, and I grew up believing I was. The bartender could be forgiven for not realising that on my mother's side, I whakapapa to Ngāi Tahu. Like him, I'm not a mind reader. But in that wink, I saw an assumption: that I saw my friends as he did.

On weekdays, I teach at a school in South Auckland. I'm a new teacher; I have a lot on my mind. On Thursday lunchtimes, I have duty on the courts. My job is to be there: to keep an eye on the kids, and to intervene if necessary. An adult presence in the world of children.

A couple of weeks ago, I was watching some of my students play basketball. I was intrigued: I knew these kids from different classes, and here they were, playing together. And I was thinking about aroha, about how much I care for these kids: their smiles, their tears. As their teacher, I see the best in them. I see their potential, and I help them to imagine how they might realise it.

I also worry for them. I know that our society doesn't value our brown people as much as it should. I know that, although our diversity has made us stronger, we too suffer from the disease that afflicts so many other societies. I know that, as well as grappling with adolescence, these children are learning to grapple with racism—and that they're growing up faster than we are.

It's a painful thought: not all of my students will reach their potential.

It's a thought I choose to sit with, though, because it's a necessary one. It helps me to explain to myself why it's so important that we stand up to racism. The reason is that if we don't, we're accepting a less-than-perfect world for everyone, including our children.

The fact is, ethnicity still determines a person's opportunities in life: Māori and Pasifika generally experience worse outcomes than Pākehā in education, health, and our justice system. To not care about this is to accept it. This is why we must stand up to racism when we witness it: because ethnicity shouldn't determine these things.

We need to re-think how we view this problem. We tend to think of racism as something that only affects certain people, and the risk here is that those of us who aren't targets are able to ignore it. I've written recently about he tōrangapū aroha, the Politics of Love. Aroha helps us to see that racism isn't someone else's problem: it's our problem.

When we love each other—when we care about other people—we're hurt by what hurts them, and we celebrate what benefits them, even if we don't know them personally. Aroha is the answer not because love will give us an easy fix, but because it repositions us relative to our concerns. It encourages us to see racism as our problem, and urges us to resist it.

Aroha requires us to take this one step further, though: it asks that we give each other opportunities to learn, to grow, and to move beyond our mistakes. If we don't allow people to change, how can we expect one another to grow? In our letter to the manager, Jo and I explained that, although we do not plan to return to the bar at this stage, we're open to sitting down and talking with the people who work there, if they're willing to. I really hope they will get in touch with us.

I keep thinking about the wink that the bartender gave me—about that assumed complicity, that 'us and them' way of viewing the world. When we look at racism through the lens of aroha, we realise that it isn't something that only happens to 'us', or that only affects 'them'. It's a problem that involves everyone, and we must work together to solve it.

Note: We never received a reply from the manager, and we have not returned to the bar.

7

We're Ready for Love

This article originally appeared on *The Wireless* in August 2017.

In 1881, the peaceful village of Parihaka was invaded. Fifteen hundred men, led by the Pākehā Native Minister, assaulted the Māori settlement. Its leaders were arrested, women were raped, buildings pulled down, and crops destroyed.

Two years earlier, Te Whiti o Rongomai had instructed the people to plough land that had been taken from them—an act of passive resistance against its unjust confiscation. The prophet's instructions were clear: 'Go, put your hands to the plough. Look not back. If any come with guns and swords, be not afraid. If they smite you, smite not in return. If they rend you, be not discouraged. Another will take up the good work.'

And when the soldiers arrived in 1881, Te Whiti reiterated his call for peace. As he and his whanaunga Tohu Kākahi were being led away, he spoke again to the people, telling them to be 'steadfast in all that is peaceful'.

In urging the people of Parihaka to resist injustice but insisting that they do so peacefully, Te Whiti demonstrated the basis upon which our peoples might live together in peace. Te Whiti gave us—both Māori and tauiwi—an example of loving politics that continues to inspire us today.

Max Harris and I first sketched the Politics of Love in 2015. It is a values-based politics, which affirms the importance of people and extends beyond us to non-human animals and the environment. The Politics of Love encourages us to imagine our entire politics in loving terms.

As our next general election draws closer, we are faced with another chance to make politics more loving. We're ready for love. As a nation, we need love more than ever; and we have a history of progressive policy in women's suffrage, indigenous rights, and homosexual law reform. I believe that the two biggest issues we must now address are inequality and animal agriculture. The Politics of Love insists that we engage with these issues, and suggests how we can approach them.

Inequality has become entrenched in Aotearoa New Zealand. The richest ten percent of us own more than half our nation's wealth. This is unacceptable, especially when we consider that between a quarter and a third of our children live below the poverty line, and that homelessness is at an all-time high. The suffering among our people is appalling, as is the cynicism that views it as inevitable. The Politics of Love challenges this attitude, and asks us to look for solutions. Love does not ignore suffering, and it does not resign itself to it: it insists on helping those who are in need.

When I think about inequality, I think of Michael Joseph Savage and the Social Security Act, which was adopted by parliament in 1938. Savage was a politician who, like Te Whiti o Rongomai, suffered with his people. He put his country before himself, sacrificing his health to see the successful implementation of a piece of legislation aimed at assisting the most vulnerable people in our society. His legacy—despite all the attempts at dismantling it—still stands as a bastion of hope, a symbol of what we might accomplish if we make decisions that will benefit all of us.

I am reminded, too, of David Lange and our country's anti-nuclear stance. Lange, who, like me, grew up on Māngere Road, spoke of love in his maiden speech to Parliament:

> I believe that our challenge is to create a society where people feel committed to each other, where they have an interdependence which no adversity can force apart, where they realise they have a duty to their brothers, and where the fruits of such a society are seen in the love, the charity and the compassion of the people.

Lange's own love for people of all backgrounds is legendary in Ōtāhuhu, where he lived and served. In leading our nation's anti-nuclear policy, he taught us that we can take a moral stand, even when doing so is difficult, and even where it could affect our interests. He showed us, yet again, that Aotearoa New Zealand can set an example for the rest of the world.

As we work to address animal agriculture, we might remember our anti-nuclear stance, as well as Lange's care and concern for people. Animal agriculture causes harm to animals, and it damages the natural environment—and our economy is complicit in this. As well as insisting that we treat animals with respect, the Politics of Love recognises that animal agriculture is one of the largest contributors to climate change, and that, ultimately, this will cause us to suffer.

If we are to transition to a more sustainable economic structure, we will need to transcend 'us' and 'them' politics and the 'urban/rural' divide. As well as speaking for the voiceless, we must ensure that farmers' voices are listened to, so that we can properly support each other through this challenging transition, and, together, overcome the structural barriers to change.

Although we bear many scars, our nation has a history of loving politics. If we choose to follow the example of those who cared for our people, those who encouraged us to do the right thing *because* it was the right thing, we will reclaim that history and turn it into tradition.

So, what is to be done?

Over the next month and a half, a lot of attention will be given to voting. We should remember that politics is not just about voting: it can also involve persuasion, voluntary work, formal employment, campaigning, public service, and many other forms of action.

But what about voting? What does the Politics of Love mean for *this* decision?

When people ask me what guidance the Politics of Love offers, I explain that the first thing it asks of us is that we care: about each other, and about politics. When it comes to the election, we need to take our choice seriously, and involve ourselves in the debates. Then, we need to vote.

'Yes,' you may be thinking, 'but *how* should I vote?' I will not endorse one party over another. And I will be among the first to say that just because a politician mentions love does not mean that their politics is loving: during his campaign for president, Donald Trump repeatedly referred to love—as when he declared his love for Mexico—while pushing a politics of fear.

The Politics of Love asks us to look beyond words and vote on values. Loving values, such as *compassion*, *responsibility*, and *trust* are central to this politics. We can judge a party's values by its policy proposals, its past policies and their outcomes, as well as by its politicians' words and actions. The Politics of Love urges us to judge these lovingly and vote accordingly.

You might ask yourself, 'Which party will do the most to realise what is best for all of our people, for non-human animals, and for the natural environment?' I cannot answer this question for you. You must engage with the debates, and make the decision yourself.

The Politics of Love is within our reach. We are ready for loving politics, and the history of our nation gives us inspiring examples to follow.

It is up to us, now, to realise it.

8

Realising the Politics of Love

This article originally appeared on *Impolitikal* in August 2017.

Many of us are longing for a more caring world. The Politics of Love gives us hope that we might realise it. How will we realise loving politics, though? What is to be done?

The Politics of Love is a values-based politics, which affirms the importance of people and extends beyond us to non-human animals and the environment. It asks us to re-imagine our entire politics in loving terms. The Politics of Love is radical—it remains open, and includes all of us—but it is not extreme. It takes as inspiration the loving acts that permeate and transcend our day-to-day interactions. It asks only that we love.

So, what is to be done?

The first requirement of the Politics of Love is that we care: about politics, and about each other. It is always as individuals as we act, whether alone or as part of a collective. For this reason, we must resist apathy—as well as the idea that, as individuals, we cannot change politics. Importantly, we need to recognise that these two attitudes reinforce each other.

We also need to re-think our understanding of politics. bell hooks, in discussing loving politics, refers to the idea of a 'love ethic'. All politics is ethical. Politics concerns those of our actions, and those dimensions of our actions, that involve others. The Politics of Love requires us to recognise our interdependence; and as love is *universal*, it asks us to extend our concern—beyond ourselves and those closest to us, to *all* people, as well as non-human animals.

It is important, too, that we think about power. There is no shortcut to this. We must learn about power relations, and how these operate to marginalise and exclude people. Part of this understanding can come through experience, and part of it will come through dialogue. Listening is the best way to learn—as is reading. Among the thinkers whose works have helped me begin to think about power are Linda Tuhiwai Smith, Peggy McIntosh, and Ta-Nehisi Coates.

And we must act. We should try to work together—because loving politics is relational, and because collective problems, such as climate change, require collective responses. But you should also be willing to act alone: sometimes, love asks us to do what others will not.

How you act will depend on our situation. Each of us must ask, What can I do to help realise loving politics? We tend to have rigid ideas about what political action involves, but persuasion, example-setting, voluntary work, personal projects, employment, campaigning, voting, and public service (as well as many other types of action) can all be used to realise loving politics.

Persuasion is a powerful political action. I think of the people who have persuaded me in my life. My stepmother, Kathryn Gatland, had a strong influence on the development of my political views as a teenager; her influence continues to inform how I engage politically now. And my friend Max Harris, with whom I first sketched the Politics of Love, has helped to shape my political views, through conversation and by sharing books with me.

Even more powerful than persuasion is example-setting. What we choose to eat, and not eat, is political: it involves others. I take seriously Australian philosopher Peter Singer's contention that unless you also oppose speciesism, 'no basis remains from which you can, without hypocrisy, criticize racism or sexism.' When I first heard the arguments for vegetarianism, although I found them compelling, I did not alter my eating habits. What finally convinced me to go vegetarian (and, eventually, vegan) was the example of others. These people took the time to explain their choices to me, and, more significantly, they *demonstrated* that this dimension of ethical living was viable.

You may be thinking, Yes, but how should I *vote*? It is very important that we avoid thinking that voting is what politics *is*—that if we vote, we have discharged our duty. This is, nonetheless, a crucial question. The answer, of course, will depend on where you are. But regardless of where you are, you should vote on values, because, beyond campaign pledges, values determine policy and help to shape its outcomes. We should ask each other, Which party's values are *most loving*?

Central to the Politics of Love are loving values—such as *compassion*, *responsibility*, and *understanding*. These values derive from, and are interpreted with reference to, love. You can judge a party's values, loving or otherwise, by considering its policy proposals, its past policies, and the outcomes of those policies—as well as its politicians' words and actions. If you live in a society that allows you to vote, you should; but remember that love requires more of you than this.

Finally, we must nurture our capacity for love. Many of us have been brought up to believe that love is only ever about others: other people, other beings, even—but never about oneself. This is ironic, because in order to love others, we must love ourselves. We should seek out loving people, and learn from them. We should also resist the accusation—which we often cast against ourselves—that we are unable to love. In his little book *How to Love*, Zen Master Thích Nhất Hạnh says,

> Since we're human beings, we make mistakes. We cause others to suffer. We hurt our loved ones, and we feel regret. But without making mistakes, there is no way to learn. If you can learn from your mistakes, then you have already transformed garbage into flowers. Very often, our mistakes come from our unskillfulness, and not because we want to harm one another.

When we say 'everyone makes mistakes', we remind each other that we are only human, that experience forms an integral part of our loving education, and—very importantly—

that our imperfections do not condemn us as 'unloving'. We should practice reconciliation, because, as Nhất Hạnh says, 'Your peace and serenity are crucial for all of us.' To love is to continuously strive to transcend one's imperfections, and to actively allow other people to do the same.

The Politics of Love has the potential to transform politics. Loving politics *is* achievable, but it depends on us to realise it. We must recognise the power each of us has to help create a more caring world for everyone, and we must *act*.

9

Arohatia te Reo

This article originally appeared on *The Pantograph Punch* in September 2017.

In May, I went to Ōtākou Marae in Dunedin for a kura reo—a week-long, full-immersion Māori language retreat. I was huddled up with lots of other learners eager to improve their reo. It was my fourth kura reo, but only my first in Te Waipounamu. I whakapapa to Kāi Tahu, the largest iwi of the South Island, so it was a special experience. One of the highlights was hearing the mita of the Kāi Tahu dialect. It's remarkable that after all te reo Māori has been through, it still has regional differences.

On the first day of the kura reo, we were divided into groups. The group I ended up in was unusual: it was comprised half of adults, half high school–aged children. Whenever I meet children who speak te reo, I make the most of it. Their reo is often better than mine, and talking to them is a good test: your reo either cuts it, or it doesn't. It's wonderful to learn from young people—and it got me thinking that our education system could better nurture our children's rangatiratanga in the revitalisation effort.

I was still thinking about this when I got back to Auckland. I believe te reo Māori should be compulsory in schools. It should sit alongside English in the New Zealand Curriculum—as it does in Te Marautanga o Aotearoa, the Māori-medium curriculum—and it should be nurtured in all our children, at all levels of education.

This argument hasn't made much headway. It quickly comes up against the retort that making te reo compulsory would cause students to resent it. Comedian Dave Armstrong deconstructs this claim in a recent piece of satire. Writing from 2057, he tells us to accept that 'the English language is dying'. After all, he says, no one speaks it anymore:

> In New Zealand, Asian and Pacific languages are far more prevalent in our big cities. Txtreodarin is by far the biggest written language amongst teenagers, and since te reo Maori was made compulsory in the 2020s, Maori is the language of the countryside.

He criticises the 'dreamers' who think English should be compulsory, saying:

> New Zealand once had a visionary Education Minister called Hekia Parata who famously said, 'compulsion breeds contempt.' If we force children to speak English then surely they'll resent it? Though it's interesting how Parata only said that compulsion

breeds contempt when talking about compulsory Te Reo Maori, not other compulsory subjects like Maths or Science.

When the proposal that we make te reo Māori compulsory is given serious consideration, we tend to think of the practicalities. There's a lack of teachers who are qualified to teach the language, and our national qualifications don't adequately reflect the diverse levels of exposure that different learners have had to it. With time and effort, though, these problems could be addressed. One academic recently suggested it could take as few as nine years to develop the teaching capacity for all our students to be taught te reo Māori from Years 1–10; and we could adjust our qualifications to reflect children's diverse starting points.

The bigger question is: why? Why should our indigenous language be given precedence over other subjects—over other languages, even—especially when studying other subjects, such as Chinese, could bring economic benefits?

The answer is that te reo Māori will make us stronger as a people. *He iwi kotahi tātou.*

Thinking about the Politics of Love helps us to see this. The Politics of Love, which I first sketched with Max Harris in 2015, emphasises *togetherness*, and so has a strong focus on community. Recognising the importance of all people, it insists that we're stronger together.

Learning te reo Māori promotes togetherness. It fosters understanding between people, expands our appreciation of relationships and the responsibilities we have for each other, and deepens our knowledge of the origins of Aotearoa New Zealand and our place in it. It also enables us to better understand Te Tiriti o Waitangi, including its significance for tō tātou reo rangatira. (The Māori-language version of the Treaty is integral to the document. The Waitangi Tribunal and the Courts both found that the government's responsibility to actively protect te reo Māori was established with the signing of Te Tiriti o Waitangi—and the government itself recognised this obligation in 1997.)

Te reo Māori is more than a language: it's a link to an enduring worldview, connecting people and peoples, past, present, and future. If more of our rangatahi were learning te reo, our communities would become interwoven, and our nation would be even stronger.

As a second-language learner, I've encountered diverse perspectives, formed strong relationships, and started to reconnect with my own Kāi Tahutaka. I've also begun to explore my European heritage. And I've witnessed friends from many backgrounds—both Māori and tauiwi—grow into themselves, learning to appreciate the similarities and differences in our diverse experience.

Valuing te reo Māori connects to valuing tāngata Māori. If Māori were better understood, and if Māori voices were listened to with the respect they deserve—if we were actively combating racism with understanding and working to decolonise our discourse as well as our institutions—we'd likely see the alleviation of many of the social disparities that negatively affect Māori whānau. Making te reo compulsory in schools is a positive step we can take to nurture our people's well-being.

Importantly, teaching te reo Māori in schools wouldn't take anything away from our children. It might in fact help our tamariki learn other languages. Rather than choosing between Māori and Chinese, for example, learning te reo could enable them to better engage with other languages and cultures, nurturing them as they grow into citizens of the world.

Making te reo Māori compulsory would also assist with its revitalisation. The biggest challenge for those of us who cherish te reo Māori is to find a reason for all New Zealanders to learn it. Tā Tīmoti Kāretu, the tohunga reo, argues that Māori must lead the revitalisation effort:

E kore te reo e mate noa i a ia anō engari ka mate nā te korenga o te iwi nōna taua reo i aro atu ki te pupuri, ki te āta tiaki, ki te kōrero. . . . [N]ō reira, e te ao Māori, kāti te ūpoko mārō, te māikoiko, te toupiore ki te kore hoki koe te Māori e hāpai ake mā wai kē? Mā Pākehā? Ko au e kī ana engari mō tēnā!

And he's right. At present, it's Māori who are most invested in our reo rangatira; if we don't stand up for it, we can't rely on other people to do so.

In thinking about how to revitalise te reo Māori, we might think about te reo Pākehā. English is considered essential for communication here in Aotearoa New Zealand and internationally, and it's the language in which most of our politics and business are conducted. Those who aspire to power speak English; indeed, it was its association with power that led to its rise in the nineteenth century. Te reo

Māori, by contrast, is perceived as having little value because 'it isn't spoken overseas', and it isn't as obviously connected to economic growth as other languages are.

Those of us who already value te reo Māori and would see it survive have a responsibility not only to speak it, but to find a compelling reason (or, better yet, reasons) for its being spoken. This reason must speak not only to us, but to other people as well. I don't think it's necessary to view te reo Māori in terms of *power*, as such, but we do need to be able to say why it's important.

One reason for valuing te reo Māori is that it can be understood as integral to our community and fundamental to our understanding of ourselves. Te reo Māori is unique to Aotearoa New Zealand; it is part of what makes us who we are. In this way, te reo Māori is one of the pou supporting our nation. It can also help individuals to understand themselves: learning te reo Māori encourages each of us to establish a connection, or connections, to the land. It is a taonga for all New Zealanders, and it enables all of us to understand ourselves *as* New Zealanders.

In his book *Ka Ngaro Te Reo: Māori Language Under Siege in the Nineteenth Century*, Paul Moon points out that schooling played a significant role in the decline of the Māori language and the ascendency of the English language. Given that schooling played such an important role in the rise of English in this country, it's reasonable to think that it could assist in the revitalisation of te reo Māori. And given the violence with which the language was treated in schools—punishing students for speaking their reo in schools was government policy well into the twentieth century, with painful consequences not only for those who were abused but for the language itself—this is the site where reparations should be made. Considering the reach of education, teaching te reo Māori in schools seems like the best option available to us.

There are people who insist te reo Māori has no real value. However, those who argue against learning it have, generally, had very little exposure to it. There are others who say that focusing on community is something we should move away from, that people should look out for themselves. But this way of relating to the world is incoherent: it holds that people are better off alone, when really we're interdependent. All of us rely on other people; it's only fair to acknowledge this, and that, given our interdependence, compassion is indispensable. *Fairness* and *compassion* are values that bring us back to love—and love leads us to community.

In loving te reo Māori, we'll make Aotearoa New Zealand a better community.

10

What Is Love and How Can It Benefit Politics?

Sarah Illingworth and Philip McKibbin

This conversation originally appeared on *Impolitikal* in October 2017.

Sarah: You recently wrote a piece for us about the Politics of Love philosophy you've developed with Max Harris. I'm interested in this as I grew up in the Christian church, and learning to understand what love is, and how to practice it has always been very important to me—if elusive at times! It seems almost too straightforward though, to say 'if people were more loving, politics would work better', partly because how people understand and express love varies widely. For example, I understand the willingness and ability to engage in healthy conflict to be a crucial element of love, but others see any kind of conflict as symptomatic of love's absence.

Which isn't to say I think humans should live in a state of conflict, or seek conflict for conflict's sake, but that in a strong relationship—whether platonic, professional, or romantic—you should feel safe to be honest and confront problems, and if the relationship can withstand that and last, it deepens. To me that's more loving than ignoring problems and allowing them to get worse. It's also more likely to lead to positive change and growth. How do you understand love, and what aspects of love do you think politics would benefit from engaging?

Philip: It's interesting that you say you came to an understanding of love through your involvement in the church. Although I'm not a Christian, my understanding of love is informed by the New Testament, and the Gospels in particular.

I agree that how we define love is very important, and I've experimented with a few different 'definitions'. When Max and I first sketched the Politics of Love, we conceived of love as 'a sentiment of enduring warmth'. While Max has continued to write about love as a 'deep warmth directed toward another', I've come to think of love in different terms. I've explored formulations like 'love is the will to love', and 'love is for love, and, being love, is for people'; although these are somewhat circular, I think they capture something of what love is.

I've settled—temporarily, I suspect!—on thinking of love as a combination of care, concern, and commitment. I'm also enchanted by the idea that 'love' is irreducible, that we cannot get away from the word itself. I agree with your suggestion that honesty is very important. One of my favourite thinkers, bell hooks, emphasises the importance of honest communication in her writing about love.

I think love can be fierce, but it's also inclusive. If 'conflict' is to be constructive, it needs to be underpinned by love. This is, I think, the role that love should play in politics: it should underpin our decision-making, informing our entire politics. The challenge is to develop an understanding of love that can do this successfully.

Sarah: Agreed! It's love's complexity that gives it its deep power. I like your description of love as a combination of care, concern, and commitment, in part because it hints at my belief that we need to get away from the idea that love is a passive thing. The right kind of friction can lead to resolution, and change—although there's always a risk there will be hard losses along the way.

You're right, the friction needs to be constructive or you end up back with politics-as-circus. Approaching politics from this perspective could go a long way to resolving seemingly irreconcilable issues. Diplomatic organisations like the UN have a reputation for tiptoeing around tricky issues rather than actively addressing and resolving them.

To me, that's un-loving. If love confronts, it does so with the intention of resolution and growth—progressive change—although, as noted, this isn't always a comfortable process. Love doesn't ignore a wound and leave it to fester; it seeks to remove the source of infection and treats the wound so it can properly heal.

And sure, maybe you're left with a scar, but scars are what history's made of. Of course, in terms of world politics the fallout, and scars, from addressing some 'wounds' can be immense. Can you describe how a Politics of Love would work in application? How do you enact a loving politics without either being too passive, or so confrontational that you start WW3?

Philip: Absolutely—I think love can definitely help us to heal wounds. And it's that understanding, that love is underpinning the process, that gives loving politics its power to resolve disputes. How does the Politics of Love work in application? The Politics of Love asks us to care. We also have to want to find solutions to our problems, though. (A lot of disputes remain unresolved because people care about particular issues, but aren't willing to do what's necessary to move forward.) I'm wary of giving blanket statements about how the Politics of Love works in practice for two reasons.

The first is that I don't have all of the answers: the Politics of Love is open and inclusive, and it urges all of us to engage in it collectively. The second is that every problem is unique, and, as such, has its own solution. The Politics of Love does give us guidance, though. It's a values-based politics: it encourages us to use values such as *compassion*, *understanding*, and *trust* in our decision-making.

I've written elsewhere about how love might help us to address terrorism—it's all about healing those wounds. More recently, I've been thinking about leadership. With the departure of Barack Obama as president of the United States, the lack of leadership globally on issues such as climate change, nuclear weapons, and women's rights has become painfully clear.

The Politics of Love urges us to stand up for values such as *fairness* and *responsibility*, and to do what we can, where we can, to promote constructive dialogue and positive action.

The key to avoiding WW3 (so to speak) is dialogue. We need to eschew the pettiness—the bickering, the name-calling—that has come to characterise politics. Instead, we should be honest, understanding, and respectful. (It all comes back to values!) We must constantly ask ourselves, What is the point of politics? I believe it is to create a better world for all of us.

Sarah: And that should happen in very practical ways. I've written previously about my frustration with the petty name-calling and rhetoric of politics, and might just go ahead and quote myself here:

> The way I see it, the public sector exists to manage the resources of a place in such a way that all who live in that place have an equal chance at having a good life, and are fairly treated while they go about it. Government is about the management of people and practicalities so we can all do our thing, and enjoy our time on the planet we've found ourselves on. It shouldn't be about overinflated personality and rhetoric, and parliamentary spats that make bratty children look polite.
>
> The good news is, there are many people who do work in the public sector in a helpful way. Who are politically and socially engaged not for change-the-world brownie points or rule-the-world motives, but because they know it's something some of us have to do. These people may be visible, and they may be invisible to you. They might work in high profile roles,

or quietly behind the scenes at schools, community centres, NGOs, or in local government. They might be practitioners, academics, teachers, nurses, journalists—and they are probably underappreciated and underfunded.

Basically, I believe the role of government is to manage the public sector in a way that is as fair and efficient as is practicable. For example, through ensuring that roles such as those listed above—charged with such a huge responsibility for social well-being—are well-resourced and supported, and that all members of the public are able to access the routes via which they can meet their basic needs.

When ex–Green Party co-leader Metiria Turei acknowledged she'd lied[4] to increase the benefit she received earlier in her life, as a single mother, I thought: Here's a woman who has experienced firsthand the limits and consequences of a system designed to protect the interests of a different kind of person to her. She chose to be honest, and to wear the fallout, in the hope it might highlight the pressures that people in similar circumstances are dealing with.

To me that act is far more loving, far more authentic, than many of the other political antics we see play out.

 Golriz Ghahraman ✓
@golrizghahraman

A woman bares her scars to highlight the pain of others. History & the disaffected will recall @metiria differently than the vicious pundits

1:28 AM · 9 Aug 2017

4   www.theguardian.com/world/2017/aug/09/new-zealand-green-party-leader-metiria-turei-resigns-lied-to-claim-benefits

Metiria risked her career and her status in the hope it might dismantle some of the systemic barriers that people with low incomes face in New Zealand, and lost her job because of that. If acting out of love in the political arena puts people in a position of vulnerability, how do we protect them?

Philip: Turei is someone who has led, and who continues to lead, in a loving way. What she did took courage, which is, in my view, an essential aspect of loving action. How do we protect those who enact loving politics? We stand behind them, and make our support for them felt, not only by those leaders, but also by 'the vicious pundits' (to use New Zealand Green Party MP Golriz Ghahraman's phrase) and those who would follow them. More broadly, our challenge is to ensure that the risks these loving leaders take, and the consequences they suffer, benefit those they are standing up for: whether those are individual people, communities, non-human animals, or the natural environment.

The risk Turei took was losing her ongoing, positive influence as co-leader of the Green Party. It's up to us, now, to ensure that that risk and the consequences she suffered were worth it. We owe her that, and we owe it to the people whose situations she highlighted. This is something we must do together, and with a Labour-led government we now have a real chance of success.

Collectivity is another dimension of loving leadership, and can help to ensure that politics is, as you say, fair and efficient. It isn't only as individuals that we lead. We can also lead as communities, small and large—as vegetarians and vegans do for animals and the environment, for example, and as Aotearoa New Zealand has on a range of issues, such as women's suffrage, indigenous rights, and homosexual law reform. This is one of the insights that the Politics of Love brings with it, and I think it helps to show why love is indispensable when it comes to politics.

11

The Prophets of Love

This article originally appeared on *Impolitikal* in February 2018.

One assumption that people often make about the Politics of Love (usually in criticising it) is that it is a religious framework. Often when I'm discussing it with people, they'll speak of love as if it cannot be divorced from religion. The assumption seems to be that because I take love seriously, I must have assumed a Christian worldview—or be about to!

I've felt the urge to defend the Politics of Love against this misunderstanding, partly because I'm suspicious of organised religion, but mostly because I think this characterisation of it is inaccurate, and that, as a result, the criticisms directed at it are misguided. I've sometimes deliberately avoided mentioning religion in setting out the Politics of Love so as not to suggest an association between the two, lest what I say be misinterpreted.

Nonetheless, religion and—more broadly—spirituality have informed my understanding not only of love, but of politics as well. As a teenager, I attended King's College, an Anglican secondary school, where I was taken with Rev. Murray Bean's sermons on love; and as a young adult, I completed my Master of Arts in Philosophy, looking at the relationship between well-being and spirituality from a political perspective.

Those who know me best appreciate the contradiction between my strong interest in spirituality, and my deep, often very vocal, opposition to religion. I remain uncomfortable with the anti-intellectualism that Christianity propagates as well as the pseudo-intellectualism it allies itself with: in both cases, to ensure its survival, whatever the cost.

I still see beauty in the conception of love expressed in the Gospels, though.

When I read, as an adolescent, how Jesus instructed us to turn the other cheek, to give up our cloaks as well, to carry that load even further; when he told us, 'You have heard that it was said, "Love your friends, hate your enemies." But now I tell you: love your enemies and pray for those who persecute you. . .' the truth in his words was self-evident. And when he admonished our hypocrisy—'How dare you say to your brother, "Please, let me take that speck out of your eye," when you have a log in your own eye?'—it was as if he was telling us that we should be good simply because to be unloving is incoherent, *dishonest.* . . .

I realised, eventually, that not everyone understood the reasoning behind Jesus' words as I did: that, unless it were taken very figuratively, 'love your enemies and pray for those who persecute you *so that you may become children of your Father in heaven*' gives a clearer, yet murkier reason for loving:

because 'God' wills it, just as he could easily have willed us to be unloving. But insofar as Jesus *does* emphasise love above all else—and when I'm feeling charitable, I believe that he does—I consider him a prophet.

Although the conception of love underpinning the Politics of Love has been informed by the New Testament, the Politics of Love does not justify itself with reference to religion. Love can be understood independently of religion. For this reason, it should be acceptable to atheists and agnostics like myself, as well as Christians and people of other religions.

Critical thinking—like other forms of intellectual engagement—has a central place in the Politics of Love, because it enables us to evaluate the strengths and weaknesses of ideas. It requires that we analyse problems carefully, and develop genuine, lasting solutions to them. As individuals, we must also develop the capacity for intellectual honesty. We must learn to pursue the conclusions of ideas, however uncomfortable doing so is in practice, and have the courage to revise our beliefs when their implications prove false or inconsistent.

Which is to say, we must be willing to reject harmful ideas. When I think of honesty and what it requires of us, I think of George Orwell, Arthur Koestler, and Albert Camus, who were, initially, seduced by communism, but were later among the first to speak out against it when they realised that communism had become inextricably linked with murder. They had the courage to revise their views—very publicly— and at great cost to themselves.

When I think of the Politics of Love and those historical figures who gave expression to it, I think especially of Martin

Luther King, Jr. and Te Whiti o Rongomai. Honesty has encouraged me not only to recognise these two leaders as spiritual figures, but also to acknowledge the role of spirituality and religion in their politics—and to explore the relationship between that spirituality and the loving dimension of their politics.

Martin Luther King, Jr. is regarded as one of the great moral and political leaders of the twentieth century. Although he is thought of by some (including myself) as a prophet, the spiritual dimension of his leadership is sometimes overlooked. But Dr. King was, very famously, a Baptist minister, and his religion infuses every aspect of his politics.

The relationship between his religious and political views is especially evident in his sermon 'Loving Your Enemies', which is collected in his beautiful book *Strength to Love*. Here, he declares that loving one's enemies is key to solving the problems of the world. 'There will be no permanent solution to the race problem,' he tells us, 'until oppressed men develop the capacity to love their enemies.' And he is very clear as to *why* we must love our enemies. It is not simply because doing so will solve our problems; it is 'because only by loving them can we know God and experience the beauty of his holiness.' Whatever your take on his religious views or his politics, he saw the two as inextricable.

Another spiritual leader whose politics was loving is Te Whiti o Rongomai, the man of peace who was born in battle. With his whanaunga Tohu Kākahi, Te Whiti founded the Māori settlement at Parihaka, in Taranaki. There, he led his people in passive resistance against the unjust confiscation of their land. He instructed them to plough the land that had been taken from them, erect fences, and remove surveyor's pegs. The village of Parihaka suffered for its stand, but the words and actions of its people continue to inspire those who work for peace today.

Te Whiti was identified in his youth as a prophet, and he used spiritual language to bring people together. 'Come to me all those who have understanding and faith,' he said. He compared his people to the tribes of Israel; and in the days leading up to the invasion of Parihaka, he echoed the words of Jesus: 'I am here to be taken. Take me for the sins of the island. Why hesitate? Am I not here? Though I be killed I yet shall live; though dead, I shall live in the peace which will be the accomplishment of my aim.'

But Te Whiti was also a critical thinker. Dick Scott's book *Ask That Mountain* recites the prophet's response to accusations that his people had forsaken religion:

> We have been blamed because we have no church and do not pray but I say that prayer is useless and resultless and no man was ever benefited or healed by prayer. Given two men, one of whom shall spend the night in prayer and the other shall sleep with his wife, notice the two results in the two cases. The first's efforts are entirely without tangible results whilst the latter, without mentioning the pleasure that accrues, has a prospect of an increase in his family for his reward. We are all in the same hole and the rain wets the praying and prayerless alike.

While I am not a religious person, I would describe myself as spiritual. I recognise in the words and actions of these prophets something of what I have experienced since I was very young. I have had experiences which are not easily describable, which I believe to be significant, and in which I have recognised something of what love is. I have described the sensation as 'a feeling', knowing that this descriptor is inadequate. When I have tried to explain it in more detail, other people have told me that they have experienced something similar.

I remember experiencing this when I was a little boy. And when I listened to Rev. Bean's sermons in the King's College chapel, I felt the same sensation, more powerfully. It was only later, however, as an adult, that it occurred to me to think of it as spirituality. What is this 'feeling'? What, exactly, does it 'feel' *like*? Perhaps you, too, have experienced it. It is empowering, energy: it tells me that there is something to be done, that I must do it. . . .

I think that spirituality *can* inspire loving politics, and I think that the words and actions of Martin Luther King, Jr. and Te Whiti o Rongomai prove this. Their politics was loving because it sought to remedy injustice, because it rejected violence, and because it expressed a commitment to inclusive solutions. In both cases, their politics was also underpinned by engaged spirituality. It would be dishonest not to acknowledge this.

We must still be prepared to critically evaluate spiritual insights before we act on them. In order to avoid being misled by charismatic liars or fanatical demagogues, we must 'corroborate'—we must *find other reasons for*—the courses of action that they advocate, and be prepared to explore other solutions if we cannot, in honesty, locate them.

But if we are committed to doing this, we shouldn't fear spirituality.

As bell hooks writes in her wonderful book *All About Love*,

> there is a realm of mystery that cannot be explained by intellect or will. We all experience this mystery in our daily lives in some ways, however small, whether we see ourselves as 'spiritual' or not. We find ourselves in the right place at the right time, ready and able to receive blessings without knowing just how we got there. Often we look at events retrospectively and can trace a pattern, one that allows us to intuitively recognise the presence of an unseen spirit guiding and directing our path.

Rather than rejecting this intuition, we should accept it alongside other forms of creative thinking, recognise its inspirational value, and trust that critical thinking will protect us from its excesses, as we expect it to in other areas of our lives.

12

Loving Justice and Non-Human Animals

This article is based on a seminar I gave on 19 January 2018 at the fourth Minding Animals International Conference in Mexico City. I have developed its arguments in response to feedback, reflection, and further reading. However, I have attempted to retain the spirit of my presentation, because the audience and the format shaped what I shared.

Tēnā koutou. Ko te mea tuatahi, me mihi atu au ka tika ki te tangata whenua o te wāhi nei, arā ki Ngāi Nahua. Ko te tuarua, me mihi atu ki ngā tāngata katoa o Mēhiko i ō koutou manaakitanga ki a mātou. Ā, ko te tuatoru, he mihi nui ki ngā kaiwhakahaere o te hui nei, arā, o Minding Animals, i ō koutou whakaaro nui, i tō koutou aroha hoki ki ngā kararehe. Ko wai tēnei? I te taha o tōku matua, nō Ingarangi, nō Airangi ahau. I te taha o tōku whaea, nō Kōtirangi, nō Kāi Tahu hoki. Nā reira, tēnā tātou katoa.

I want to begin—having acknowledged the indigenous people of Mexico City, and all of the people of this beautiful country for their hospitality, as well as the organisers of this conference for minding animals—by mentioning my friend and fellow New Zealander Max Harris, with whom I first started writing about the Politics of Love. Max deserves a special mention for another reason: years ago, he encouraged me to become a vegetarian. Max had been a vegetarian for a while, and his example inspired me. When I finally did transition to vegetarianism—and I remember this clearly—he said simply, 'Yes, that fits.' (When Max finally goes vegan, I plan to say the same thing to him!)

What is the Politics of Love? Max and I first started developing it in 2015. It is a values-based politics, which affirms the importance of people, and extends beyond us to non-human animals and the natural environment. We think that love should underpin politics. Significantly, loving politics has precedents in the everyday acts of love we show to one another, as well as in the feminist, civil rights, and LGBTQI movements. There are many different conceptions of love, but most recently, Max and I have been discussing love as an 'attitude' or orientation—or, to use Max's term, a 'mood'. Importantly, the Politics of Love gives expression to loving values, such as *understanding*, *responsibility*, and *trust*. These values derive from love, and love enables us to interpret them and hold them in balance.

Let me briefly say what this talk is *not*. It is not an analysis of the concept of love—you're going to have to indulge me at certain points. It is not an explanation of the Politics of Love, either. It isn't even an account of loving justice.

Rather, I want to humbly offer six 'suggestions', which I hope will prompt discussion.

Suggestion 1: Animals should have a central place in the Politics of Love.

My first suggestion is that animals should have a central place in our politics.

The dominant conception of justice ignores animals. Liberalism, which achieves its clearest expression in the contractarian theory of John Rawls, treats animals as an afterthought—insofar as it considers them at all. I think it is telling that, in Rawls's original position, it is humans who are situated behind the veil of ignorance, and that they choose what is best for themselves. Rawls says in *A Theory of Justice* that justice as fairness (and 'rightness as fairness'),

> would seem to include only our relations with other persons and to leave out of our account how we are to conduct ourselves toward animals and the rest of nature. I do not contend that the contract notion offers a way to approach these questions which are certainly of the first importance; and I shall have to put them aside.

But the Politics of Love *cannot* ignore animals; it cannot put them aside. The suffering that they experience cries out to us, and it is this concern which focuses our attention. This insight—that it is their capacity to experience pain that forces us to consider them—was captured by Jeremy Bentham, who wrote, '... the question is not, Can they *reason*? nor, Can they *talk*? but, Can they *suffer*?'

Central to the Politics of Love is the notion of equality. I follow bell hooks, and understand love as anti-racist, anti-sexist, and opposed to all forms of domination. In her book *All About Love*, hooks writes, 'Domination cannot exist in any social situation where a love ethic prevails.' I think we need to accept speciesism as a form of domination, and recognise its relationship to other forms of discrimination. As Peter Singer writes in *Animal Liberation*, unless you also oppose speciesism, 'no basis remains from which you can, without hypocrisy, criticize racism or sexism.' Alice Walker echoes this sentiment when she writes, 'The animals of the world exist for their own reasons. They were not made for humans any more than black people were made for whites or women for men.' The Politics of Love, then, is anti-racist, anti-sexist, *anti-speciesist*, and so on.

I think 'interests' is a particularly useful term for thinking about our obligations toward non-human animals, for two reasons. First, it can accommodate differences among animals—both species and individuals. And second, it conceptualises animals' needs positively rather than negatively: rather than focusing exclusively, or even primarily, on suffering, it has a broader focus, encouraging us to ask, 'What is *good for* them?'

There are two important concepts that relate to interests: consciousness and sentience. Consciousness is significant, because it underpins subjective experience. Although it can be difficult to say what provides evidence of consciousness, as Thomas Nagel writes in his essay 'What Is It Like to Be a Bat?', 'fundamentally an organism has conscious mental states if and only if there is something that it is like to *be* that organism—something it is like *for* the organism.' Similarly, sentience is important because it is here that experience is concentrated. According to Helen Proctor, 'Animal sentience refers to the ability of animals to experience pleasurable states such as joy, and aversive states such as pain and fear.' Sentience can be difficult to prove, but the problem of proving that, say, a pig is sentient is not that different to the problem of proving that your neighbour is sentient. (Is a pig squealing when it is manhandled all that different to your neighbour describing how much it hurt when he was assaulted?)

I contend that if the Politics of Love takes animal interests seriously, it will, at least, be opposed to the suffering that we as humans inflict on non-human animals, and may even entail positive responsibilities toward them. Importantly, this is consonant with loving values, such as *compassion*, *gentleness*, and *mutuality*, all of which are integral to this politics.

Suggestion 2: Animals should be included in politics differently to humans.

My second suggestion is that human and non-human animals should be included in politics in different ways.

Even though the argument for including animals in our politics is made in relation to human concerns (e.g. anti-racism), the struggle is different. In thinking about inclusion, it is helpful to think about voices. In combating racism, sexism, and most other forms of human oppression, we need to make space for voices that are not being heard. This is a very different project to *speaking for* others. In combating speciesism, however, animals need to be given a voice. This *does* require us to 'speak for' others. (It is worth noting that many animals do have voices—for example, a cat's purring. We need to listen to these. But we also need to do a lot of the cognitive and linguistic work for them. Animals need interpreters.) These two projects can learn from each other, but they are different.

Suggestion 3: The place of animals in politics should be differentiated.

My third suggestion is that animals should occupy different places in our politics.

Not all animals are the same; they have different interests. This can be seen at the species level; it can also be seen at the individual level. We must also avoid falling into the trap of thinking that similarity to human beings can serve as a proxy for determining a species' moral worth. This is especially tempting if the focus is on consciousness or sentience, because we find it a lot easier to imagine other mammals and birds as conscious and sentient as we are than we do, say, fish or insects. But animals that are dissimilar to us in many other ways also exhibit these traits. In her excellent book review 'The

Sucker, the Sucker!' Amia Srinivasan explores the experience of octopuses. 'Octopuses almost certainly feel pain,' she tells us: they nurse and protect injuries, they have complex sensory capacities, they have large nervous systems, and they show complex behaviour. She goes on:

> They are sophisticated problem solvers; they learn, and can use tools; and they show a capacity for mimicry, deception and, some think, humour.... Their intelligence is like ours, and utterly unlike ours. Octopuses are the closest we can come, on earth, to knowing what it might be like to encounter intelligent aliens.

The intelligence of octopuses is especially remarkable given that the last common ancestor between other intelligent animals (humans, monkeys, dolphins, dogs, and crows) and octopuses 'was probably a primitive, blind worm-like creature that existed six hundred million years ago.'

As I have already indicated, I believe we should think in terms of interests, because this way of conceptualising our responsibilities toward animals is sufficiently complex to accommodate differences between them. I also think that we should be willing to allow space for that which we do not understand.

In 'What Is It Like to Be a Bat?', Nagel conducts an important thought experiment: he tries, and fails, to imagine what it is like for a bat to be a bat. He says that he can imagine having webbing on his arms, flying around at dawn and dusk catching insects in his mouth, having poor vision, perceiving the world through echolocation, and hanging upside down during the day. However,

> [i]n so far as I can imagine this (which is not very far), it tells me only what it would be like for *me* to behave as a bat behaves. But that is not the question. I want to know what it is like for a *bat* to be a bat. Yet if I try to imagine this, I am restricted by the resources of my own mind, and those resources are inadequate to the task. I cannot perform it either by imagining additions to my present experience, or by imagining segments gradually subtracted from it, or by imagining some combination of additions, subtractions, and modifications. . . . So if extrapolation from our own case is involved in the idea of what it is like to be a bat, the extrapolation must be incompleteable.

We cannot extrapolate from our own experiences in order to fully understand what it is like to be another animal. We cannot imagine what it is like for another to be them. We can *empathise* with animals other than ourselves, both human and non-human—but empathy, too, has its limits. As Lori Gruen writes in her book *Entangled Empathy*:

> When we empathize with others we are attempting to imagine fully how they experience their situation from their position. We notice the environmental cues that

they are responding to, and we try to understand their particular frame of mind. However, their perspectives are often shaped by experiences that we ourselves haven't had, and thus our empathetic engagement will be limited or incomplete.

Just as I cannot know what it is like for you to be you, we cannot know what it is like for a bat to be a bat, or a pig to be a pig, or a shrimp to be a shrimp. So we need to ensure that loving justice allows space for our uncertainty, so as to adequately accommodate differences between species and between individual animals. I call this the 'difference principle' (!). We cannot know if a spider feels alarm, but if a child chases one with her finger, he acts like he does. (At least, the small spiders we have in New Zealand do!) Significantly, we may never know whether or not he does. But the fact that we cannot describe or understand a phenomenon does not mean that we should just disregard it. As Nagel writes, 'to deny the reality or logical significance of what we can never describe or understand is the crudest form of cognitive dissonance.'

Suggestion 4: Loving justice should actively concern itself with the alleviation of suffering.

My fourth suggestion is that loving justice should work to alleviate suffering.

It is generally agreed that love concerns itself with suffering. That love 'moves toward' suffering is reflected in loving values, such as *concern*, *forgiveness*, and *mercy*. I understand love as *opposed to* suffering. It is for this reason that loving justice is opposed to retribution and revenge. These concepts entail the infliction of suffering, and are irreconcilable with loving justice.

The alleviation of suffering is one of two 'ends' toward which justice might be directed. We can think of these ends as 'principles' of justice, proximity to which can be used to judge the relative justice of a community or political system.

As Jeremy Bentham argued, there is no logical reason to distinguish between human suffering and that of non-human animals. And the sheer scale of animal suffering is appalling. According to Compassion in World Farming, more than seventy billion animals are reared for food globally each year, and the vast majority of these are kept in awful conditions. Given the equivalent moral weighting of human and animal suffering—given, that is, our commitment to anti-speciesism—the suffering of animals should be included here, at the foundations of justice. I suspect, however, that it will have to be limited, at this point, to the suffering that we inflict on animals. Even after much debate, it is not clear what our responsibilities to wild animals should be; there are, however, compelling reasons for thinking that we should leave them alone. We have not shown ourselves to be especially good at acting in other animals' interests—let alone determining what their best interests really are.

Animal suffering is *the* ethical problem of our time. As Kim Stallwood writes in his book *Growl*, 'We are their injustice.' (He goes on to say, 'Indeed, I often think that how we treat animals is so immeasurably and unbelievably exploitative that we are beyond any scale of justice.') The harm that is currently inflicted upon animals helps us to see that a justice that ignores animal suffering cannot be considered loving.

Suggestion 5: Loving justice should have a second 'end', which we might think of as the promotion of human dignity. As well as the alleviation of suffering, loving justice might concern itself with the promotion of human dignity. 'Dignity' is a problematic concept. I, for one, am deeply suspicious of it. *Star Trek: Deep Space Nine* fans will be familiar with the Ferengi 'rules of acquisition'. (The Ferengi are a species of alien who are totally obsessed with profit, and their rules of acquisition are, essentially, scriptural edicts.) My favourite is rule #109: 'Dignity and an empty sack is worth the sack.' Nonetheless, I think the word can help us to understand this second 'end'.

By 'human dignity', I mean our relational humanity. This includes our relationships not only with each other, but also with non-human animals and the natural environment. Our humanity is influenced by the non-human world around us, but it also includes human concerns, or 'preoccupations'. Among these are the desire to be more loving, and a strong interest in the realisation of justice.

I believe that loving justice can, legitimately, promote specifically human concerns insofar as these do not negatively impact animals (or, do not cause or contribute to animal suffering). It can do this because justice is a human endeavour: it is created by and for us. But this does not mean it is amoral, or that 'anything goes'. Justice, and the politics that informs it, sits within a broader ethical framework; and this politics, like ethics, needs to be 'coherent' if it is to have normative force.

Suggestion 6: Indigenous peoples might lead us in reimagining justice for animals.

Finally, I want to suggest that indigenous peoples might lead us in reimagining justice for animals. There are two reasons for thinking that we are uniquely placed to do this.

First, we understand the importance of living in harmony with the natural environment. In his book *Tikanga Whakaaro*, Cleve Barlow explains the Māori concept of aroha, which is usually translated as 'love':

> He aha te aroha? Ko te aroha he tikanga whakaaro nui; ka aroha tētahi tangata ki tētahi tangata, ki tōna iwi, whenua hoki, ki ngā kīrehe, ki ngā manu, ki ngā ika, ki ngā mea katoa e tupu ake ana i te whenua. Ka aroha te tangata ki tētahi atu, ahakoa he aha tōna āhua i roto i ōna pikitanga ake, i roto anō i ōna heketanga iho, i roto i ōna hari, i roto i ōna pōuri, i roto i āna mahi pai me āna mahi hē.

> What is aroha? Aroha in a person is an all-encompassing quality of goodness, expressed by love for people, land, birds and animals, fish, and all living things. A person who has aroha for another expresses genuine concern towards them and acts with their welfare in mind, no matter what their state of health or wealth.

As Barlow explains, aroha extends beyond people to land, and to animals, birds, fish, and everything that grows upon the land. To love is to express one's concern to them.

Second, we are sensitive to issues of power. Indigenous peoples are intimately acquainted with oppression, and we have devised and refined ways to resist it. Importantly, these different oppressions are connected. Marjorie Spiegel notes:

> [A]ny oppression helps to prop up other forms of oppression. This is why it is vital to link oppressions in our minds, to look for the common, shared aspects, and fight them as one, rather than prioritizing victims' suffering. . . . For when we prioritize we are in effect becoming one with the oppressor. We are deciding that one individual or group is more important than another, deciding that one individual's pain is 'less important' than that of the next.

These two facts—that we understand the importance of living in harmony with the environment, and that we are intimately acquainted with oppression—give us strong reasons for thinking that indigenous peoples are uniquely placed to lead in reimagining justice for animals.

Before I conclude, I would like to invite you to contribute to the development of this theory. The Politics of Love does not belong to one person, or even to two. It is actively inclusive, and it needs all of our knowledges. *Aroha mai, aroha atu.*

Hei kupu whakakapi: i toro atu au ki Mēhiko i runga
i te whakataukī nei:

Unuhia te rito o te harakeke, kei hea te kōmako e kō?
Kī mai ki ahau, 'He aha te mea nui o te ao?' Māku e
kī atu, 'He tangata, he tangata, he tangata!'

Heoi, kua mōhiotia: ehara i te mea nui 'te tangata, te
tangata,' engari ko te aroha e.

13

Love, Politics, and Veganism

Carla Alicia Suárez Félix and Philip McKibbin

'Love' has re-entered our political vocabulary. In Aotearoa New Zealand's recent general election, the Green Party campaigned on love, with co-leader James Shaw declaring, 'I'm proud to lead a party that stands for the politics of love and inclusion, not hate and fear.' When the Green Party formed a coalition with the Labour Party, Prime Minister Jacinda Ardern announced that the government would be 'empathetic'. In Mexico, after last year's devastating earthquake, people banded together in solidarity with one another, against the lack of love shown by the government. And in the United States of America, a #LoveArmy, led by CNN political commentator Van Jones, has risen to resist the hate that has allied itself with Donald Trump. Worldwide, 'love' is being used to promote inclusivity: to rally people for gay rights, as we saw with the slogan 'Love Wins', and to resist discrimination directed against people, including women, ethnic minorities, and refugees.

One area of concern still receives little attention, however, and that is animal welfare. This is remarkable for several reasons. More than seventy billion animals are raised for food every year (that's around ten times as many animals as there are people living on the planet), and the vast majority of these live their lives in appalling conditions. On top of this, our use of animals is having a catastrophic impact on the natural environment. Animal agriculture is among the leading causes of climate change. So far, politics has failed to address this.

The Politics of Love gives us hope. New Zealanders Max Harris and Philip McKibbin first sketched this theory in 2015. It is a values-based politics, which expresses values such as *kindness*, *responsibility*, and *trust*. The Politics of Love is actively inclusive, affirming the importance of people, and extending beyond us to non-human animals and the natural environment. That love should inform politics has precedents in the kindness we show one another in our daily lives, as well as in the feminist, civil rights, and LGBTQI movements.

When we think about our treatment of animals, it is difficult to see how it could be considered loving. The seriousness of the problem is especially evident when it comes to our use of animals for food: the poultry industry, which rears more than fifty billion birds (the vast majority of whom are raised in appalling conditions) every year for meat and eggs pales only in comparison to our inhumane treatment of cows, who are repeatedly impregnated so that they produce milk, only to have their calves torn from them at birth. But the problem extends far beyond our diets. Most of us wear animals: on our feet, around our waists, on our wrists. We use them in a variety of other ways: as parts and ingredients, for testing, for entertainment, to carry us, and to carry our things. This not only causes suffering; it involves the subordination of other sentient beings.

And when we think about love, it becomes very clear that all of this is unacceptable. Love is a way of orienting oneself, or a political community, to the larger world. It can be thought of as a combination of care, concern, and commitment, and it is inclusive of all. Our understanding of the concept is informed by bell hooks, who characterises love as anti-racist, anti-sexist, and opposed to all forms of domination. In her book *All About Love*, she declares, 'Domination cannot exist in any social situation where a love ethic prevails.' Peter Singer's work on animals helps us to see that our treatment of animals constitutes another form of domination. In *Animal Liberation*, he states that unless you also oppose speciesism, 'no basis remains from which you can, without hypocrisy, criticize racism or sexism.'

Love 'moves toward' suffering—it concerns itself with it—as loving values such as *compassion* and *mercy* help us to see. To ignore the suffering of animals would, then, be *un*loving. To continue to insist that we have a right to subordinate other sentient beings would be inconsistent with a conception of love that rejects all forms of oppression. When this is understood, it becomes clear very quickly that something must change.

This change must start with our diets. Since Carol Hanisch published her paper 'The Personal Is Political' in 1970, most feminists have asserted that the personal is, indeed, political: issues that are generally understood as personal, such as domestic work, reproductive decisions, and child-rearing, involve power relations, and for this reason should be understood as political. In her article 'The Personal is Political: Feminism and Anti-Speciesism', philosopher Catia Faria extends this slogan to include what we eat. When we think about all of the implications of this 'simple' decision, we realise that it is not merely a personal choice: it has huge implications for the environment, for people, and—most significantly—for other sentient beings. In order to mitigate these harms, we must resist animal agriculture.

Vegetarianism is not enough. It is true that the suffering involved in meat production is abhorrent, and that by transitioning from an omnivorous diet to a vegetarian one an individual can drastically reduce the amount of suffering she enacts. Simply by ceasing to eat pig meat, for example, she will avoid contributing to the unnecessary suffering of these remarkably intelligent, highly social animals. However, the suggestion that by cutting meat out of her diet she is no longer complicit in animal suffering is false. A diet that no longer contains animal flesh, but includes, for example, eggs, dairy, and gelatine, still involves unnecessary suffering. If she is truly committed to avoiding unnecessary suffering, this individual will transition to veganism—a diet that eschews *all* animal products.

As millions of vegans worldwide are demonstrating, fears that we cannot thrive—let alone survive—without eating animal products are unfounded. Numerous organisations, including the British Dietetic Association and the American Academy of Nutrition and Dietetics, now recognise vegan diets as suitable for every age and stage of human life. We can nourish ourselves without engaging in the unnecessary harm that animal agriculture necessitates.

However, vegan diets do not completely avoid harm. Lori Gruen, a prominent ecofeminist, reminds us that even vegan diets necessitate the suffering and death of sentient beings. She writes:

> Living today, even for vegans, involves participating unwittingly in the death of sentient individuals. . . . We harm others (humans and non-humans) in all aspects of food production. Many are displaced when land is converted for agricultural purposes, including highly endangered animals. . . . Animals, birds, and insects are killed when fields and plants are harvested. Though it is hard to calculate the harms to human and other animals from climate changes as a result of greenhouse gas emissions from the agricultural sector, it is impossible not to contribute to these harms and still eat. Vegan diets are less harmful than those that include animal products, to be sure, but the harms and deaths occur nonetheless.

Rather, veganism involves a commitment to avoiding harm wherever possible. Recognising the moral centrality of veganism is necessary if we are to avoid domination. As Alice Walker has written, 'The animals of the world exist for their own reasons. They were not made for humans any more than black people were made for whites or women for men.' Veganism is the best way to resist speciesism—and it is much more than a personal decision. Understood as part of a loving political movement, it can help us to realise a less discriminatory and more fair society for all. Veganism, not vegetarianism, then, must be understood as the 'moral baseline' to which we should aspire.

It might be thought that we should simply leave animals alone—and in some cases, this may very well be the best course of action, especially when it comes to wild animal populations whose lives are not significantly impacted by human activity. But we want to suggest that, instead, we should cultivate loving relationships with animals. Just as children often take it upon themselves to nurse injured animals back to health, and similarly to how many of us have developed loving relationships with companion animals, we should develop loving ways of relating to animals. These relationships will take many forms, but they should demonstrate care, concern, and commitment. Veganism, with its commitment to reducing suffering wherever possible, can be understood as one facet of a loving orientation toward the non-human world.

As we have mentioned, love is not indifferent to suffering. Instead, it works to alleviate it. This is an area in which our spiritual traditions give instruction. Many diverse traditions advocate compassion for non-human animals. Perhaps the best example of this can be found in Jainism. In this tradition, all life is considered sacred and inviolable. Mahâvîra, a Jainist teacher, claims in the *Âkârânga Sûtra* that:

All beings are fond of life, like pleasure, hate pain, shun destruction, like life, long to live. To all life is dear. . . . All breathing, existing, living sentient creatures should not be slain, nor treated with violence, nor abused, nor tormented, nor driven away.

Jainism even has a ritual for repenting transgressions, which involves asking for forgiveness from all living beings. The idea that we should show compassion toward all forms of life is, then, not exclusive to veganism; it forms an integral part of longstanding human traditions. Nor is it sentimental; compassion is an act of love toward life itself.

Another spiritual figure who advocated compassion toward non-human animals was Mahātmā Gandhi. He preached non-violence, and insisted that the key to this was abandoning our own comfort for the sake of others—including non-human animals.

Gandhi promoted what we would now call a vegan diet (the word 'vegan' had not been coined then). And in the conclusion to his *Hind Swaraj*, he expressed his opposition to vivisection, or performing experiments on living animals. Gandhi thought materialism led to a lack of morality. Today, we can see that our so-called 'progress' has been built on the corpses of nature—humans' and non-humans'. Gandhi, like Te Whiti o Rongomai before him and Martin Luther King, Jr. after him, showed us that non-violence can be more persuasive than violence. He believed that violence and evil are mutually reinforcing, and that non-violent resistance was the way to fight evil.

The Politics of Love does not exalt self-sacrifice. It does, however, insist that we act against injustice. We must work to be just ourselves, and we must stand up to the injustice of others. We can do this by refusing to participate in harmful practices (for example, by refusing to drink cows' milk), by actively supporting the development of alternatives (for example, by switching to plant-based milks), and by engaging in other forms of strategic action aimed at exposing and overcoming exploitation (as, for example, Farmwatch, which conducts covert, often illegal, surveillance of farms, and which sometimes rescues animals, does in Aotearoa New Zealand).

Significantly, the Politics of Love gives expression to loving values, such as *mutuality* and *moral courage*. These can guide us as we work to realise love individually and collectively—and it is values like these that lead us to veganism.

We believe that different forms of discrimination are interconnected, and that they must be addressed together, which is to say that we look at speciesism through the lens of intersectionality. For example, we think that feminism without veganism is incoherent. Anti-sexist movement risks being undermined by speciesist ideology if we as feminists do not also condemn the oppression of non-human animals. In *Feminist Theory: From Margin to Center*, bell hooks writes:

> Individuals who fight for the eradication of sexism without supporting struggles to end racism or classism undermine their own efforts. Individuals who fight for the eradication of racism or classism while supporting

sexist oppression are helping to maintain the cultural basis of all forms of group oppression.

We know that some people will take exception to our assertion that you cannot be truly anti-sexism without also being anti-speciesism, just as some people still believe it is possible to be anti-racism while holding on to sexist ideas. We know that this claim will upset some people; we understand that it is confrontational. We make it deliberately, because positive change will not occur without confrontation. As feminists, we stand in solidarity with those people who are struggling against gender oppression. Our intention is not to minimise the work that has been, and is being, done to promote gender equality; rather, we are arguing that the feminist project will not fully succeed while other forms of oppression remain unchallenged.

Our argument is confrontational in another way. Some people find it offensive to compare human suffering with that of non-human animals. Marjorie Spiegel, in her book *The Dreaded Comparison*, writes on human and animal slavery:

Comparing the suffering of animals to that of blacks (or any other oppressed group) is offensive only to the speciesist; one who has embraced the false notions of what animals are like. Those who are offended by the comparison to a fellow sufferer have fallen for the propaganda spewed forth by the oppressors. To deny our similarities to animals is to deny and undermine our own power. It is to continue actively struggling to prove to our oppressors, past or present, that we are similar to our oppressors, rather than those whom our oppressors have also victimized. It is to say that we would rather be more like those who have victimized us, rather than like those who have also been victims. Let us remember that to the oppressors, there is often very little difference between one victim and the next.

As feminists, we understand the importance of confrontation to advancing social change. When women gained the vote in Aotearoa New Zealand in 1893—among the first in the world to do so—this success was attributable, in part, to confrontation: persuasion, protest, and petitions. As we continue to struggle against oppression, we must resist the cultural amnesia that characterises domination and privilege. We will not apologise for being confrontational, because we understand it as positive and necessary.

Importantly, this confrontation must be non-violent. The Politics of Love recognises that constructive dialogue and action are superior to violence, which causes suffering and often reproduces dominant hierarchies. We must ground our resistance in non-violence—regardless of whether it is for humans or non-humans. A contemporary example of non-violent resistance is the Black Mambas, an all-female, anti-poaching, paramilitary patrol. These women, recruited from local communities in South Africa, protect rhinoceroses and elephants from poachers, armed only with pepper spray and handcuffs. Every month, they spend twenty-one days patrolling on foot or by jeep at dawn and at dusk, looking for traps and footprints and listening for gunshots and other suspicious activity. This resistance group has contributed to a 76 percent reduction in poaching since 2013.

Increasingly, animal advocates are recognising the need to highlight the connection between our exploitation of animals and other forms of exploitation. In his excellent book *Growl*, Kim Stallwood writes:

> Long a moral crusade, animal rights now needs to be a political movement as well, embedding itself fully within other social justice movements and drawing inspiration, support, and knowledge from the other activists. Advocates need to engage in these other struggles, not merely because it's the ethical thing to do, but because we need to show that our struggle is the struggle of these other social movements and their coalitions *as well*: that animal rights is their fight, too. We've long expressed our bafflement at how other social movements fail to 'get' that animal rights is a social justice concern. We need to *show* them that animal rights is also about fighting food insecurity, protecting the environment and biodiversity, and opposing sexism, racism, homophobia, and other forms of prejudice.

Some people mistake concern for animals as being against people. Far from being 'anti-people', the Politics of Love affirms the importance of people. It recognises the parallels between the way we treat animals and how we treat each other. As Carol Adams writes in her essay 'What Came Before The Sexual Politics of Meat: The Activist Roots of a Critical Theory', 'incorporating animals into the dialogue and activism of social change doesn't eliminate humans from concern; it just reassembles the players by disempowering that human/animal boundary that enforces oppression.'

The Politics of Love holds that people are, essentially, noble. We believe that most, if not all, people want to be good, and actively strive to do the right thing. We think that, just as most of us don't want to be racist or sexist, when they appreciate the connection between these forms of oppression and speciesism most people won't want to be speciesist either.

In his little book *How to Love*, Zen Master Thích Nhất Hạnh argues that when we hurt others, often it isn't because we intend to hurt them, but because we are unskillful:

> Very often, our mistakes come from our unskillfulness, and not because we want to harm one another. I think of our behaviour in terms of being more or less skillful rather than in terms of good or bad. If you are skillful, you can avoid making yourself suffer, and the other person suffer.

Veganism requires us to develop what we might think of as 'loving skills'—that is, skills which enable us to act in loving ways—including, for example, the ability to select vegan products, which involves knowing what to look for, and the capacity to prepare nourishing vegan meals. It also requires us to develop *sensitivity* to the suffering of others (which might also be thought of as a loving value).

Importantly, the Politics of Love is understanding. It does not hold our past mistakes against us. Informed by the values of *understanding*, *forgiveness*, and *humility*, it seeks to contextualise harmful behaviour, recognising that there are many factors informing our capacity to love.

Lori Gruen makes a related point in explaining her stance on veganism:

> Though most of us can readily eschew animal parts in our own diets, ecofeminists are mindful of the violence perpetuated in many gendered, racialized, and colonial contexts as well as the realities of a changing climate and thus forgo top-down, absolute universalizing judgments that everyone, everywhere should see 'veganism as a moral baseline.' Instead, most ecofeminists argue for 'contextual moral veganism' that recognizes both the moral centrality of a vegan diet and contextual exigencies that impede one's ability to live without directly killing or using others.

The Politics of Love is not blind to the circumstances in which we live our lives. Rather, it is forward-looking, focusing on creating conditions under which we can express love. Unfortunately, many people feel threatened by veganism, because it implies a moral judgment, and because its steadfast opposition to harmful practices is often mistaken for a condemnation of the people who participate in those harms. The Politics of Love does not seek to condemn people, and it is not interested in punishment. Rather, it asks us what we will do *now*, for love, to make our world a better place for all of those who share it.

14

Love Is Not About 'Other People'

No, love is not about other people. Not always, anyway.

Love is becoming a radical force in politics. A #LoveArmy, led by Van Jones, was formed following the election of Donald Trump; the fiftieth anniversary of the assassination of Martin Luther King, Jr. in 2018 has led to a renewed discussion of his ideas of civic love; and Bishop Michael Curry explored the concept in his sermon on the power of love at the May 2018 wedding of Meghan Markle to Prince Harry of the British royal family.

But many of us are confused about what the word means.

The idea that love is 'all about' others is widespread. It connects to another problematic concept: self-sacrifice, or the idea that, to be a good person, one needs to surrender one's own interests. But many thinkers have argued that *self-love* is necessary if we are to love others. In her book *All About Love*, feminist theorist bell hooks writes, 'Self-love is the foundation of our loving practice. Without it our other efforts to love fail.' And Zen master Thích Nhất Hạnh expresses a similar sentiment when he says, 'If you are a true friend to yourself, you can be a true friend to a loved one.' Rather than being 'selfish', self-love is extremely important.

In 2015, Max Harris and I sketched the Politics of Love, a values-based politics, which is actively inclusive, opposed to domination, and committed to equality. Since then, the Politics of Love has been described as 'a politics of other people'— and I can understand why. The idea that love encourages us to see beyond our own concerns and re-centre those of the community is one that I agree with. Love asks us to care, and to care about more than just ourselves. However, I worry that when we see love as being 'about' other people, we elevate their needs above our own, and we risk viewing the important work of self-love as unnecessary, or harmful. There are further problems with thinking about love in terms of other people, so I think our traditional conceptions of love need revising.

Just as the Politics of Love challenges us to re-think what counts as political action and re-examine how we as individuals relate to each other and our communities, it asks us to re-think who and what love concerns. Love's first concern is those who suffer—and many of those aren't people. The scale of animal suffering eclipses that of human suffering. More than ten times as many non-human animals as there are people living on the planet are being raised by us for food, and the vast majority of them are being kept in appalling conditions and killed in cruel ways. If love 'moves toward' human suffering, surely it moves toward animal suffering as well. Love for animals is *as* legitimate as love for people. And as Peter Singer writes in *Animal Liberation*, unless you also oppose speciesism, 'no basis remains from which you can, without hypocrisy, criticize racism or sexism.'

I think that love could also guide our relationships with the natural environment. It has been said that, 'When you like a flower, you pluck it; but when you love a flower, you water it.' I believe that loving values such as *gentleness* and *kindness*, as well as our nurturing capacities, could be extended to the non-sentient world. I suspect that we will eventually see the true strength of our love in our capacity to extend it to that which is utterly unlike us—to trees, to the soil, to rain. . . . If loving politics can include the environment, this could give hope to a planet grappling with climate change.

These diverse concerns converge in veganism. The Vegan Society defines veganism as 'a philosophy and way of living that seeks to exclude—as far as is possible and practicable—all forms of exploitation of, and cruelty to, animals for food, clothing, and any other purpose.' But vegans will tell you that non-human animals aren't the only ones to benefit from veganism: it's also great for your health, and that of the planet. Both the American Academy of Nutrition and Dietetics and the British Dietetic Association affirm that vegan diets are suitable for every stage of human life, and in 2010, a United Nations report, 'Assessing the Environmental Impacts of Consumption and Production: Priority Products and Materials', suggested that a global shift toward meat- and dairy-free diets was necessary to save the world and its people from the catastrophic effects of climate change.

Love is not about 'me', and it isn't about 'them'; it's about *us*.

When I ask myself what love requires and open my heart to the answer, it encourages me to open my heart to the universe itself—and to care about everything in it.

So let's be more imaginative! Love isn't *just* about other people.

15

The Love Economy

Take a second: think about the economy.

What comes to mind? Money? Work? Wages?

Inequality? Unemployment?

Poverty?

Now, try to imagine something different—something *viable*, but different. It's hard, isn't it? It's not that alternatives haven't been floated. (I mean, we're all familiar with the basic tenets of communism—common ownership, 'from each according to his ability, to each according to his needs', etc.). It's that most of those that *have* been proposed have been 'discredited', or aren't viewed as feasible.

But maybe—just maybe—something else is going on here. Perhaps there's another explanation for why we find it so difficult to imagine other economic possibilities.

In his book *Ill Fares the Land*, historian Tony Judt argues that, for thirty years, we've 'made a virtue out of the pursuit of material self-interest'. And now we know how much things cost but we don't know what they're worth. Something is seriously wrong with this—yet we're unable to come up with alternatives. 'This, too,' he writes, 'is something new.' People used to ask questions, debate alternatives, imagine a better world. . . . But we don't do that anymore. Something about the current economic order—neoliberalism—seems to be preventing us from inventing alternatives.

Neoliberalism—with capitalism, which underwrites it—has its own, seemingly coherent logic. I say *seemingly* coherent, because there are a lot of things that don't withstand critical scrutiny . . . like the fact that, as individuals, we don't all start from the same position, or that our planet doesn't have unlimited resources. As importantly, it centres us as atomised units, offering enough compensation (in the form of material goods and power) for placing our faith in it, that most of us do so. The result is that we not only find it difficult to imagine new possibilities, we actively resist them.

Don't believe me? Try this. Say I were to suggest that our economy could be loving—that *love* could underpin it. You'd laugh at me. 'How could economics *possibly* be loving?' But the idea itself might not actually be ridiculous. I mean, you haven't even heard it yet. It could be brilliant.

Go on, indulge me. You've come this far!

I imagine an economy with love at its centre. It would care about all of us; it would show concern for, and give special attention to, those in need; and it would take a committed, long-term view of what is 'good for' us. This economy would rely on values such as *fairness*, *responsibility*, and *trust* at least as much as—maybe even *more than*—money and material markers of wealth.

Perhaps you're thinking, 'Sure, but that would be unworkable.'

And you might be right. But what does 'unworkable' mean? And what would 'workable' look like? Is our current system 'workable'? If we look at it closely, there's a lot that *isn't* working. All of us agree that child poverty is appalling; yet here in Aotearoa New Zealand, more than a quarter of our kids are living in poverty. Are you really convinced that the system is working for them, or do you suspect that things could be better? What about the tens of thousands of people who are currently homeless—who are living on the streets, in their cars, and in garages? Is it working for them?

The neoliberal economic order isn't just failing our people. It's also complicit in our abuse of non-human animals, as well as our degradation of the natural environment. As a nation, Aorearoa New Zealand has allowed itself to become dependent on farming. As a result, almost half of our greenhouse gas emissions come from animal agriculture. Do we really believe that the current system is working, or do we just favour it because we aren't brave enough to look for alternatives? (As Albert Camus wrote in a notebook, 'There is always a philosophy for lack of courage.')

'Fair enough,' you might say. 'But what would a loving economy actually look like?'

Economics is connected to politics. If we want to know what a loving economy might look like, we can begin by asking another question: What would a loving *society* look like?

My friend Max Harris and I have already had a go at this. A few years ago, we sketched the Politics of Love, a values-based politics which highlights loving values like *compassion*, *mutuality*, and *understanding*. Since then, we've been developing it. We believe that love challenges us to re-think what counts as politics, in line with the feminist slogan 'the personal is political'. It also urges us to re-think how we 'do' politics: it advocates respectful exchange and genuine collaboration.

When I ask myself what the Politics of Love would look like if it were realised, I imagine a society in which everyone feels secure, nourished, and able to relate in meaningful ways to those around them. In such a society, we wouldn't have to worry about not having our basic needs met; we would respect and nurture the many individuals and diverse communities which comprise us; and we would have genuine opportunities to live stimulating lives that engage our strengths and talents.

It's possible that you're already living such a life. Unfortunately, many people aren't. (If we tend to forget this basic fact, it's because our privileges obscure it from us.) It's vitally important that our society works for everyone, because no child deserves to be born into inequality.

So, in such a society, how would the economy be different?

In his book *The New Zealand Project*, Max Harris includes a chapter on loving politics and work. Among his proposals is a universal basic income, a benefit paid to every member of a community regardless of their state of employment. He contrasts this with an insecure work benefit, the main aim of which is to get people into employment. 'A universal basic income best gives effect to a politics of love,' he writes. 'It expresses confidence in people's ability to determine their own life courses, rather than demeaning or belittling them.' This, he argues, is equivalent to showing love to people. He suggests that a universal basic income could enable people to leave abusive relationships by creating financial independence, allowing them to 'realise love more fully' in their own lives.

A loving economy would, as Max suggests, value more than just money. Tony Judt notes that 'wealth' needs redefining, and numerous thinkers have developed indices for measuring markers of well-being. American philosopher Martha Nussbaum's Capabilities Approach, for example, attempts to understand what is good for us holistically, highlighting 'functionings' such as *bodily health*, *affiliation*, and *play*.

What if we took this further, and instead of relying on monetary motivations—instead of *funding* initiatives—we found ways of supporting kaupapa with other-than-financial investment? If an organisation was pursuing a project—a wānanga, say, or a building complex, or an exhibition—it might call for non-monetary contributions of all kinds: food, labour, land, etc.; and with those resources, the needs of the organisation, as well as those of the community it was serving, could be fully met. Such an approach would require a lot of trust—and a fair bit of getting used to! But it wouldn't simply *rely* on love: it would also generate the love needed to sustain it, as we re-learnt reciprocity.

In Aotearoa New Zealand, this way of thinking about economics has pre-European precedents, and in the wake of treaty settlements, many Māori tribes are exploring ways of returning to traditional values. My iwi, Ngāi Tahu, has been attempting to merge these with contemporary imperatives. Its commercial endeavours, which are grounded in our cultural values, are aimed at promoting tribal development, and work to provide opportunities—in education, for example—and support, such as benefits, to its members. Its financial approach is sensitive to the wider economies within which it operates, and to which it contributes. This sense of purpose, the sharing of benefits, and sensitivity, are characteristics that we might expect to see in any loving economy. (I'm not uncritical of my iwi's model: animal agriculture and fishing, in which we invest, have no place in a loving economics.)

If we want to change our economy, we need to change the way we talk about it. As well as making space for vibrant new ideas, we need to get involved in the various debates. We must resist the neoliberal idea that only 'experts' in economics are able to comment on economic matters. (John Key cultivated an all-too-reassuring image of himself as an expert on the economy during his tenure as Prime Minister, to the detriment of democratic deliberation.) We need to hear many different voices—especially those that, traditionally, have not been listened to on economic issues.

We must continue to challenge the idea that our current economic system is the only viable one. Who among us is really willing to accept that what we have now is 'good enough' for our people, non-human animals, and the natural environment? Are you? Or are you as outraged as I am that 290,000 Kiwi kids are living in poverty? Whatever your initial impression of 'the love economy', I hope you will agree that something needs to change—and join those of us who are working to generate ideas.

16

An Ever-Expanding Circle

Love has captured our political imaginations. In Aotearoa New Zealand's most recent general election, the Green Party campaigned on love, with co-leader James Shaw declaring, 'I'm proud to lead a party that stands for the politics of love and inclusion, not hate and fear.' (It's no coincidence that when it formed a coalition with the Labour Party, Prime Minister Jacinda Ardern declared that her government would be 'empathetic'.) In Australia, MP Andrew Leigh has spoken on the Politics of Love. And in the United States of America, love is being touted by protestors and comedians as the antidote to Donald Trump's divisive politics.

Love is, essentially, about relationships. It's about how we relate: to ourselves, to each other, and to the wider world. It is this which accounts for its popularity—and this which gives rise to a lot of confusion. (When we think about relationships, most of us think of *romantic* relationships, but love isn't just about romance. In fact, many of our ideas about romantic relationships, especially those involving ownership and control, are actually at odds with love.) When we remember this—that love is basically about relationships—its implications for how we do politics become clearer.

The Politics of Love reaffirms the feminist slogan 'the personal is political'. It encourages us to understand politics as involving all of our decisions and interactions: from what we choose to eat, to how we distribute household chores; from the ways in which we talk to each other, to the kinds of work we strive to do. It also challenges us to re-think how we talk about political issues. It guides how we talk about policy—as, for example, when we justify welfare and benefits not in terms of encouraging re-entry into the workforce, but as expressions of our commitment to those who require support. And it asks that we engage with each other respectfully. The Politics of Love recognises that reasonable people have different opinions on many different issues, and that name-calling, hate speech, and other forms of divisive language will not foster the goodwill, trust, and willingness to collaborate that are required in order to arrive at genuine solutions to complex political problems.

There are those who doubt that ideas like love can motivate political change, but social movements such as the feminist and LGBTQI movements reveal just how powerful such ideas can be. These movements have used ideas to secure real change, for people and for politics: from widespread condemnation of domestic violence, to the legislation of marriage equality. Love is one of these ideas. It has the capacity to motivate changes in attitude as well as in policy. (I am not claiming that all feminists see political currency in love—as many don't—or that all of those belonging to the LGBTQI community view our use of the term 'love' as aligned with their causes. Some queer theorists, for example, portray love as an ideology that promotes conformity to heteronormative conceptions of self and relationship.)

What does 'love' mean for our political relationships? Fundamentally, it means embracing inclusiveness over exclusion. It means moving beyond understanding relationships in terms of 'me and him', or 'us (and not her)', or 'us but not them'—and seeing the 'we' in everything we do.

Two modern social movements have expanded our understanding of what love is: polyamory and the animal liberation movement. Polyamory, which is often described as 'ethical nonmonogamy', is generally understood as the practice of having multiple partners. However, Deborah Anapol, in her book *Polyamory in the Twenty-First Century*, writes that 'polyamory has more to do with an internal attitude of letting love evolve without expectations or demands that it look a particular way than it does with the number of partners involved.' Polyamory challenges the pervasive idea that love is limited, that in order to love one (such as one's partner) or even more than one (such as our own children) we need to close ourselves off to loving others (other people's partners, for example; or other children as much as we love our own). Polyamory is radically inclusive in theory and in practice. In practice, it often involves intimacy with more than one person, it seeks out ways of communicating that nurture unity, and it has even led to more widely distributed parenting practices. In related ways, polyamorous theory is sensitive to diversity and difference, and it interrogates exclusionary relational attitudes such as possessiveness and jealousy.

Similarly, the animal liberation movement challenges our beliefs about who matters and how we should relate to others. It urges us, for example, to recognise speciesism as another form of discrimination, not unlike racism, sexism, and classism. In his book *Growl*, animal activist Kim Stallwood argues that it is love which will enable us to realise justice for non-human animals:

> Are we willing to love those we don't know or have never seen? It seems an impossible task. Yet this is what it will take to know truth, feel compassion, live non-violently, and embrace justice.

And in the conclusion to his collection *Circles of Compassion*, Will Tuttle discusses veganism—or, the practice of abstaining from animal products—and the inclusiveness that underpins it:

> Veganism demands us to question absolutely everything in us that has been modelled by our cultural programming, and to bring our thoughts and deeds into alignment with a radically more inclusive ethics that calls for respect and kindness for all beings, including our apparent opponents. We see that veganism, as boundless inclusiveness, is the essence of all social justice movements, and that it is the antidote to what ails our world.

These two movements—polyamory and the animal liberation movement—challenge the idea that love needs to, or even should, involve exclusion, and they suggest that true love is inclusive.

Still, many people argue that societies, and even one's own sense of self, depend on exclusion: that without 'the other', we would be unable to articulate who we are, or what holds us together. However, this view obscures the limiting dichotomies that exclusion necessitates, as well as the harms that it enacts. In his article 'The Enduring Solidarity of Whiteness', Ta-Nehisi Coates highlights the connection between social exclusion and solidarity: '[Sexism is] a means of forging solidarity among "men," much as xenophobia forges solidarity among "citizens," and homophobia makes for solidarity among "heterosexuals."' He helps us to see that exclusion usually underpins inclusion—and that this often involves domination. We must reject the idea that domination makes us who we are.

Love teaches us to see beyond our differences, but it doesn't ignore them. When we affirm love, we give our lives a meaning that all of us recognise, and which, in turn, recognises each of us. In love, we find purpose: we find each other, and a shared commitment to the world we share. When we place love at the centre, we come together without excluding, or dominating, others.

As we rewrite our political relationships, ever-expanding inclusiveness should be a central theme. Other implications of this approach could include opening our borders (even if this must be done gradually); showing manaakitanga, or hospitality, to immigrants (especially asylum seekers and other refugees, who are most in need of it); and a focus on the rehabilitation and reintegration of people who commit offences (over incarceration and—worse—capital punishment).

At a broader level, understanding the Politics of Love in terms of relationships encourages us to value, and uphold, those things which make for healthy relationships—namely, *honesty*, *communication*, and *forgiveness*. As the Politics of Love encourages us to understand the personal as political, it asks us to extend the loving skills we cultivate in our personal relationships, such as kindness, sensitivity to others' concerns, and truth-telling, to our less-intimate relationships.

The Politics of Love affirms our agency as individuals. If we believe that our societies should be loving, it is up to each of us to find ways to make them more loving. We must dedicate ourselves to the difficult work of love. Albert Camus reminds us that, to be taken seriously, philosophers must be willing to 'preach by example'. Love, like life, makes philosophers of us all.

17

The (Transcendental) Power of Love

Many people think of politics as being primarily about power. This is not a recent idea. Niccolò Machiavelli famously reduced politics to power; and Friedrich Nietzsche's more nuanced 'will to power' was manipulated by the Nazis, who put it to hateful ends. Today, both thinkers are admonished for their views; however, the idea that politics is essentially about power manifests in more subtle ways. Critical interrogations of power and related concepts, such as privilege, oppression, and ownership, dominate political discourse, especially within the academy. These ideas have entered our conversations: 'mansplaining' and 'hepeating', for example, are now commonly used terms to describe how men exercise rhetorical power.

Around the world, love is challenging political power. It is not merely redistributing it, which is a shared aim of the Black Lives Matter and #MeToo movements; it is also confronting assumptions about what power *is*. More and more, we are hearing the slogan, 'Love trumps hate!', especially from protesters in the United States. It is tempting to take this as an empty platitude, or an almost-clever play on words. (Shouted slogans can sometimes sound hollow.) Really, it signals a shift in consciousness: it is an expression of love's 'power' *not only* over hate, but over power itself.

In December 2017, soon-to-be U.S. Congressional candidate Alexandria Ocasio-Cortez tweeted, 'I practice a politics of love for all people.' A year later, she'd defeated the long-standing Democratic Caucus Chair Joe Crowley in a Democratic congressional primary. In doing so, she displayed what Martin Luther King, Jr. called the 'strength to love'. She reminded us that love does not defer to power; it directs it to loving ends.

Max Harris and I first sketched the Politics of Love in 2015. I believe that it has the potential to become a mighty social movement. It engages the assumption—which often remains unspoken—that politics is 'about' power. For example, it helps us to recognise a focus on the redistribution of power as 'negative': as concerned with what is *wrong* rather than with what is right, and with what *is not* the case much more than with what could be. The Politics of Love, by contrast, offers a 'positive' vision: it asks us to imagine what we might create together, and it provides a framework for developing ideas with which we will transform our societies into nurturing communities that benefit us all.

This is not to say that the Politics of Love does not recognise power. The Politics of Love is radically democratic, as it affirms the fundamental importance of our equality. It also acknowledges the urgent necessity of challenging power—as we do when we question why some people's lives are treated as more important than other people's; or why in some of our societies, it is men who make many of the important decisions over women's bodies; or when we ask why some people's knowledges and histories are privileged over others'. The Politics of Love, however, brings something more: it embraces the transcendental quality of love. It is not the case that love 'does away with' the need to interrogate power; rather, it actively facilitates this interrogation without risking the disintegration of community, and without sacrificing individuals to the collective good. Love transcends power, and power relations, by empowering those who have been disempowered, and by enabling all of us to step through power, to transform it into love for others.

A beautiful example of this occurred during the Summer Olympics in 1968 in Mexico City. In the medal ceremony for the men's 200 metres, gold medallist Tommie Smith and bronze medallist John Carlos raised their gloved fists in a Black Power salute. The image became iconic, and the two men heroes. Standing in front of the two men on the podium was silver medallist Peter Norman, a white Australian, whose quiet contribution to their now-famous salute has largely gone unnoticed. It was Norman who suggested that Smith and Carlos wear a glove each after Carlos realised he had left his at the village. He wanted to protest, too: to show his solidarity, without detracting from his friends' statement. He asked Paul Hoffman, an American rower, if he had a spare Olympic Project for Human Rights badge. Although Hoffman only had one, he took it off and gave it to the Australian. Norman wore the badge, and paid the price for it. When word of his actions got around, he was ridiculed; and despite qualifying for the 1972 Olympics in Munich, he was not allowed to attend, leading to his early retirement.

Dr. King affirmed the importance of unity, or what he called 'persevering togetherness', to dismantling oppressive systems. In his final book, *Where Do We Go from Here: Chaos or Community?*, he explains why we must work together. Not only is it pragmatic, but it gives tangible expression to the kind of society we are working to achieve. (He insisted, too, that white people's sacrifices for black civil rights should be respected. 'Consciences must be enlisted in our movement,' he says, 'not merely racial groups.') Similarly, he understood the necessity of power to realising love:

> Power, properly understood, is the ability to achieve purpose. It is the strength required to bring about social, political or economic changes. In this sense power is not only desirable but necessary. . . . One of the greatest problems of history is that the concepts of love and power are usually contrasted as polar opposites. Love is identified with a resignation of power and power with a denial of love. . . . What is needed is a realization that power without love is reckless and abusive and that love without power is sentimental and anemic.

Love, then, has a lot to do with power. To stop at power, though, would be to miss the point. Politics is not just about who has power; it is also, significantly, about what we do with it.

The Politics of Love asks that something other than power sit at the centre of our thinking. It places love at the centre—and it is from here that it elaborates itself. Refracted, love gives us values such as *respect*, *mutuality*, and *understanding*; and it is from love that we derive a concern not only for people, but for non-human animals and the natural environment as well. The Politics of Love, with its concern for all people, encourages a focus on community. Importantly, though, the conception of community that it advocates is anti-exclusionary: just as it refuses to ignore non-human animals and the natural environment, it rejects, absolutely, what Dr. King describes as 'the barbaric consequences of any tribal-centered, national-centered, or racial-centered ethic'. Loving community can be understood as an ever-expanding circle of inclusiveness, within which is a place for us all.

The Politics of Love encourages us to ask, How can we create a society that meets everyone's needs? Significantly, it suggests some answers. A loving community would ensure that everyone's material needs are met by, for example, requiring the provision of high-quality housing for all who need it. And in such a society each of us would consciously extend our social networks, beyond our families and peers, to people who we might not otherwise interact with, forming loving relationships that benefit ourselves, each other, and our communities.

I think of my friend Jeremy Roundill, or Purū, a Pākehā (New Zealand European) man, whose concern for others has led him to learn te reo Māori, the indigenous language of Aotearoa New Zealand, and get involved in activism for a range of causes that most directly affect people other than himself—including campaigning for workers' rights. In extending care to people regardless of their background, and by standing alongside our society's most vulnerable members, he embodies the community-conscious ethos of the Politics of Love.

Far from ignoring the powerless, the Politics of Love prioritises them. It gives special attention to children, who belong to our communities but who do not yet have (much) power within them. It also recognises strong responsibilities to future members, who will have to live with the consequences of our decisions, but who do not have any say in them. Indigenous thinking might guide us here. My iwi (tribe), Kāi Tahu, governs itself 'mō tātou, ā, mō kā uri ā muri ake nei' ('for us and our children after us'). Similarly, Oren Lyons, a chief of the Onondaga Nation, writes in his essay 'An Iroquois Perspective' (which is collected in *American Indian Environments*) that one of the first mandates given to their chiefs is 'to make sure and to make every decision that we make relate to the welfare and well-being of the seventh generation to come'. The Politics of Love interprets our responsibilities universally.

Politics is not primarily about power, but thinking about power highlights another important issue: it helps us to appreciate that the true site of politics is neither the seat of government nor the 'ivory tower' of the academy, but all of us, as people. A few years ago, I was working part-time as a research assistant at Te Kupenga Hauora Māori (The

Department of Māori Health), at The University of Auckland. It was there that I first became interested in the writing of bell hooks. I was researching Kaupapa Māori Theory, which meant I had to do a lot of reading. My supervisor, who was Tumuaki and Head of Department, told me to read hooks's book *Black Looks: Race and Representation*, which I dutifully did. However, I have to admit that, at the time, it did not make a strong impression on me (or, that's what I thought!).

A couple of months later, one of the office administrators stopped by my office. She told me that she had just finished reading *All About Love: New Visions*, another bell hooks book. She had been told about it, she explained, by two other women in the office. 'I think you'd like it,' she said. I took her recommendation, and I'm very glad I did. Of all the wonderful books that have helped me think through the Politics of Love, none has had as significant an influence on my thinking as that one. The Politics of Love, then, arises in the space between apathy and academia: it is less about government policy, less about inward-looking scholarly debate, and more about conversations among caring individuals; more about books that are swapped, lent, and recommended; more about our actions. . . . It is more about *us*.

Love transcends power; it looks beyond it. We know this because we witness it in our day-to-day lives: for example, when women work patiently and persistently to help men recognise and address our sexist attitudes and behaviours; and when women and men work together, in love and against patriarchy, to raise loving children, who, we hope, will have the strength to confront the many challenges that await them in the future. The Politics of Love recognises the transformative potential of love, and it encourages us to use that power to bring about a better world for everyone.

18

A Politics for the Environment

Climate change is the biggest crisis facing our planet.

The implications for our species are being widely discussed. Richard A. Oppenlander, for example, writes, in 'Our Lifeline Revealed Through the Eye of Justice', that we have reached a critical point in our evolutionary journey: we now have the power to alter our biosphere, for better and worse. 'These,' he says, 'are the very environs that sustain us and all other life on Earth. Unfortunately, we haven't acquired the wisdom or maturity to be able to manage this power in a sensible or beneficial manner.'

Many experts, moreover, are predicting that we will be the cause of our own extinction. In a recent interview, Mayer Hillman, Senior Fellow Emeritus of the Policy Studies Institute in the United Kingdom, said:

We're doomed. The outcome is death, and it's the end of most life on the planet because we're so dependent on the burning of fossil fuels. There are

no means of reversing the process which is melting
the polar ice caps. And very few appear to be
prepared to say so.[5]

Might love, which is being directed against homophobia,
racism, and sexism, help us here, as well? American philosopher
Dale Jamieson thinks that it can. In his World Philosophy Day
lecture, he argues that love can be shown to the environment—
not merely as a means to our ends, but for its own sake—and
that this gives us a strong reason for protecting it.

I believe that the Politics of Love can be a politics for the
environment.

Love is often thought of in terms of human ends. When
we talk of love for other people, the justification for extending
love beyond ourselves is often, simply, that they are people,
too. Similarly, when we talk about loving the environment,
the reasons for doing so usually relate to human interests:
for example, that protecting the planet's natural beauty will
ensure that we can continue to enjoy it, or that caring for the
environment is an expression of love for future generations
who will also depend on it. (Although these are compelling
reasons for loving the environment, they are instrumental: they
don't ask us to care about the environment *for its own sake*.)
When we extend love beyond ourselves, it usually retains a link
to people. Following Martin Luther King, Jr., Oppenlander
conceives of ethics as 'doing something for others', but he
extends this to non-human animals. He writes:

5   https://www.theguardian.com/environment/2018/apr/26/were-doomed-
    mayer-hillman-on-the-climate-reality-no-one-else-will-dare-mention

To realize justice everywhere in the world we must extend our concern well beyond the realm of the human-to-human context, or that of grass-fed, pastured, cage-free, sustainable seafood, or any other form of certified humane-raised animal or animal product.

He tells us that we should extend our concern to all 'living beings', directly *and* indirectly affected by our consumption of animals and animal products. This progressive view of ethics—as 'doing good for others'—can be understood as an extension of our concern to the non-human world *insofar as* it is sufficiently like us.

Unfortunately, though, it doesn't extend far enough.

In discussions around how to extend ethics beyond the human, there is usually a strong focus on sentience—that is, the ability to experience pleasurable and aversive states. In his book *Animal Liberation*, Peter Singer contends that,

the only legitimate boundary to our concern for the interests of other beings is the point at which it is no longer accurate to say that the other being has interests. To have interests, in a strict, nonmetaphorical sense, a being must be capable of suffering or experiencing pleasure.

This focus on sentience is important, as it helps us to clearly see how our use and abuse of non-human animals is unjust. We experience pain in similar ways, so practices which inflict suffering on other animals, which we would not also accept for human beings, are *speciesist*: they discriminate between us without sufficient reason, just as racism and sexism discriminate between people. But because the natural environment as a whole is *not* sentient, we generally fail to recognise responsibilities to it, or to its non-sentient constitutive elements, such as rivers and trees. In her book *Entangled Empathy*, ecofeminist Lori Gruen discusses this distinction as it relates to our ability to empathise:

> Loving regard for and commitment to other-than-sentient nature is part of a shift in our ethical perception . . . but it is not the same as empathy. . . . While being with or even thinking about non-sentient nature may evoke a variety of deep and meaningful experiences in sentient beings, they aren't experiences that are shared with the non-experiencing parts of the world.

This focus on sentience impacts how we think about the environment. Significantly, it limits our concern for it unnecessarily. To understand why this is, we need to think more carefully about speciesism.

The Politics of Love is anti-racist, anti-sexist, and opposed to all forms of domination. This means it is also committed to anti-speciesism. Because most of the world's suffering is experienced by non-human animals, it pays careful attention to them, via their sentience. But the Politics of Love does not interpret its anti-speciesist commitment narrowly. Its reliance on consistency helps us to see that discrimination against species with like interests is inconsistent—regardless of the species, and regardless of the interest. And to an extent, all species have common characteristics. Questions such as, 'What counts as an interest?', 'Do some of these interests pertain only to species themselves and not to their individual members?' and 'When must we take these into account?' are not ones that I will attempt to answer here. Nonetheless, at the very least, it seems clear, to me at least, that to completely disregard other species—to subjugate them, absolutely, to human interests—*is* speciesist, and wrong. When we exploit the natural environment, as many of our cultures have done for centuries now, we fail to show love to other species, sentient and non-sentient.

The Politics of Love is a values-based politics, which promotes values such as *care* and *honesty*. These values, which derive from love, guide our action. *Respect*, for example, requires us to take the concerns of other people seriously, in our day-to-day lives as well as in political debates. Significantly, we can nurture loving values. In my article 'Arohatia te reo', I wrote that te reo Māori, which is the indigenous language of Aotearoa New Zealand, should be compulsory in my country's schools. I argued that teaching te reo to Kiwi kids would promote *understanding* and *responsibility*, and that this would foster togetherness.

Love is a way of relating to the world; we can think of it as an orientation, or 'attitude'. As well as giving rise to values, love helps us to interpret, or make sense of them. How does it do this? Imagine values as stars. All of these stars are always present, even if they aren't always visible. (It is worth remembering the Māori whakataukī: *He tini ngā whetū e ngaro i te kapua iti.* 'Many stars can be concealed by a small cloud.') And some, it is true, shine more brightly than others— *kindness*, *understanding*, and *trust*, for example, outshine *anger* and *indignation*, but all have their place in the night sky. When, with open hearts, we look upwards for guidance, we are able to see what it is to love on any given night. The lover, then, is a stargazer, a constellation-maker; and what she sees is how to love. . . .

Love holds these values in balance. Let me give two examples. Just as it helps us to appreciate the need for all of us to take *responsibility* for our actions and communities, it recognises that the language of 'responsibility' has been used to demonise the most vulnerable people in our societies, and that a loving approach to social welfare issues, say, would give greater weight to *compassion* and *commitment*. Similarly, it helps us to see that, although indignation has currency when protesting Donald Trump's intended withdrawal from the Paris Agreement (because such harmful action requires a strong response), when liberal Americans talk to Trump supporters about their views, *anger* should give way to *humility*. This is because everyone deserves to be treated with respect, and because when people are listened to, and when their concerns are met, they are more likely, and better able, to express love.

Thinking critically about speciesism helps us to see beyond sentience, to 'see' all species. But I think that love can apply even more fully to the natural environment: anti-speciesism, even that which moves beyond a focus on sentience, is not the sole basis for our responsibilities to it. I think of love as expansive, and I believe that loving values such as *kindness* and *gentleness*, as well as our nurturing capacities, can be extended to all of the natural world. Importantly, this does not reduce a concern for the environment to our own interests: the focus is not only on us, or even on us and other animals, but on the environment *itself*, as well. In thinking about these relationships, we might remember the maxim: 'When you like a flower, you pluck it; but when you love a flower, you water it.'

Understood expansively, love would concern itself with all of nature, seeing beauty in moonlight, amongst the coral reefs, and sprawling across the tallest trees. . . as well as our responsibilities to them. It would de-centre us (again), allowing us to create a home in the natural world, and thereby providing a framework for finding our place in the wider universe that awaits us—a journey that we will not make if we do not first learn to love.

Attending to the natural environment could also lead us to re-imagine our societies. What if we thought of our communities as loving eco-systems? I think about the native forests in Aotearoa New Zealand, which still flourish on some of our islands. In these places, there is an abundance of fresh water and sunlight, which nourish the forests' inhabitants. If we enacted the Politics of Love in our societies, loving values would nurture us, ensuring that our needs—for food, for shelter, for company—are met. It is true that our native forests have suffered the adverse effects of mistreatment, but they still foster diverse expressions of life: they are vibrant with birds— such as tūī, kererū, and fantails—as well as tuatara, geckos, wētā, and frogs, and they host a beautiful variety of plant life, such as harakeke, kauri, and werewere kōkako.

We, too, could nurture diversity in our societies and ensure that non-human life also finds a natural place with, and alongside, us. Also, our forests have effective waste management systems. Rather than disposing of waste, they make use of it. We, too, might see value in 'negatives'—such as pain and frustration—and recognise that, with skill, these things can be used as fertiliser to help our communities flourish. Conservationists will tell you that healthy eco-systems maintain balance. In our societies, love does this.

The Politics of Love, then, is a politics for the environment. I believe that we will eventually come to see the true strength of our love as consisting not only in our recognition of all sentient beings, but in our capacity, also, to extend it to that which is unlike us—to trees, to the soil, to rain ... and, in time, outward, to the wider universe.

19

With Emotion

Julie Timmins and Philip McKibbin

Politics affects every aspect of our lives, so the Politics of Love, if it is to be truly nurturing, must take every dimension of our lives into account—including our emotions. Reflecting on emotions helps us to appreciate that the personal really is political.

Many people think that love is a purely emotional concept. It is for this reason, perhaps, that people sometimes assume the Politics of Love must only be about emotions. We strongly reject this assumption, as well as the conception of love underpinning it. That love is not only about emotions becomes clear when we think about sexism. Dismantling oppressive systems, like patriarchy, is one of the fundamental projects of loving politics, but patriarchy will not be dismantled with feeling alone: we must also think critically. We view the Politics of Love as deeply committed to intellectual engagement.

Historically, however, Western political philosophy has privileged rationality, and relegated emotions to the 'non-political'. This mirrors the public/private distinction: reason has typically been viewed as public, whereas emotion has been seen as personal, or private. And these distinctions have, of course, been invested with gender associations. Emotion has been interpreted as 'female', and reason or rationality as 'male'. As philosopher Marilyn Friedman notes, feminists have linked the denigration of emotion with the devaluation of women. 'Defending emotion, including its role in moral understanding, has become for feminists part of the project of elevating cultural esteem for women,' she writes. Although we challenge any essentialist thinking around emotion and rationality, it is important to acknowledge that this association has operated to oppress women and girls.

Feminists have also called the public/private distinction into question, and with it, the distinction between reason and emotion. Like so many of the binary impositions that we are now working to unlearn, this one no longer seems to hold. Whether or not we acknowledge it, emotions inform our thinking. Political thinking is no exception, although many people still seem to think it is. A lot of us believe we are being 'rational' in political debates, for example, when, in fact, our 'rationality' is coloured with emotion. Arguments around immigration—that immigrants will take (our taxes, our jobs, 'our' people) without contributing anything of value—are often fuelled by fear: of difference, deprivation, change. . . .

It is important that we inquire into the place of emotions in loving politics. One reason for this is that people's emotional lives are often neglected by politics. This is especially evident when we think about work. Paid work is at the centre of much public policy, including welfare. In many countries, for example, parental leave is tied to paid employment: if you are not, or have not been, working, you do not receive support. (Loving policy, by contrast, would focus on the needs of children, parents, and caregivers.) This preoccupation with paid work connects to a lack of concern for people's experience of work. The phrase 'work–life balance', which arises from this, has harmful implications: work is seen as separate to life, and correspondingly, work that is not paid—like much of the work that is done in homes, including many forms of caregiving— is not seen as real work. This phrase also suggests another problem: as paid workers are required to work more and more, less time is being left to 'life'. As a result, people's well-being, especially our emotional well-being, is neglected.

The neglect of emotional well-being is also evident in the increasing insecurity of paid work. In his book *The Precariat: The New Dangerous Class*, Guy Standing highlights the emotional consequences experienced by a growing class of people who lack labour-related security. As a result of the flexibility that has become inherent to our economic system, he explains, the 'precariat' experiences 'the four A's—anger, anomie, anxiety and alienation.' It has become extremely difficult for many people to maintain relationships and have healthy emotional lives.

Stress arises, for example, when people feel overwhelmed by their financial insecurity. They may then seek help from unethical lenders who are poised to provide a 'solution'— at outrageous interest rates. This can lead to difficulties in relationships, both within the home and outside of it. Often it is women who are left trying to create emotional stability at home, while at the same time tending to the financial burdens, many of which have arisen because a 'partner' has abandoned the family and left his debts behind. Legislation to establish fair and reasonable guidelines for lenders would do much to ameliorate this difficult situation. Addressing the underlying issue of insecurity would have an even greater impact on strengthening emotions and fostering healthy relationships.

Another reason for giving careful attention to emotions is that they can be an incredibly harmful force in politics. For example, mistrust has led to punitive welfare policies, whereby beneficiaries and their dependents are penalised for not meeting the government's expectations with little to no regard for their circumstances. It is equally true, however, that emotions can motivate positive policies: sympathy for the plight of people other than ourselves motivated the creation of social welfare systems in the first place.

In thinking about the Politics of Love, we asked each other what it is that makes emotions 'positive' or 'negative' in politics. After some discussion, we agreed that it is not something inherent to particular emotions. The idea that 'negative' emotions always have negative outcomes is untrue. Anger, for example, is generally thought of as a negative emotion—as something that we should resist—but it can prompt positive change: women's anger at being disenfranchised played an important part in bringing about universal suffrage. Similarly, fear about the harmful effects of climate change may yet encourage us to take the steps necessary to address it.

We think that what makes emotions positive or negative when it comes to politics has more to do with whether or not they contribute to everyone's well-being. This relates to how we mediate, or manage, our emotions. We believe that a concern for people—and not just some, but *all* people—is part of what love involves, and that loving action is always sensitive to its implications for other people. Love can be thought of as an orientation or 'attitude'—as a commitment, even. It is a way of relating to the world, and emotions, just like rationality, can either strengthen this relationship or undermine it. What is important is how we express our emotions. We must reflect on how and when we allow each of them to inform politics.

Importantly, politics should value our emotions. As we have already mentioned, much unpaid work is not valued. (The fact that it is uncompensated is, in our capitalist systems, itself an indicator that it is not valued.) This is especially true of many forms of caregiving. Much of this work involves emotions: the emotions of those who are doing the caring, and the emotions of those who are being cared for. This is vitally important work, as it nurtures the well-being of our people and communities. That it is not valued has negative consequences for them, and for those who do the work. In some cases, it can compromise the caregiver's quality of life. One way it does this is by taking time: caregivers who have to find additional, paid work to make ends meet are often left with very little time for the important work of self-care. This in turn impacts their ability to nurture other people.

In their book *Affective Equality: Love, Care, and Injustice*, Kathleen Lynch, John Baker, and Maureen Lyons write about the dimensions of equality that involve our needs for love and care, and the work that tends to these. They say:

Because love, care and solidarity involve work, affective inequality also occurs when the burdens and benefits of these forms of work are unequally distributed, and when this unequal distribution deprives those who do the love, care and solidarity work of important human goods, including an adequate livelihood and care itself.

It is worth noting that we see a strong affinity between the Politics of Love and the ethics of care. The ethics of care is a theoretical framework which seeks to extend 'care' from the personal into the public, while the Politics of Love centralises love, provides a space for collaborative deliberation, and manifests in diverse forms of action. Like the Politics of Love, the ethics of care affirms the importance of relationships. It also reminds us of the value of emotion. In her book *Joining the Resistance*, leading care ethicist Carol Gilligan writes, 'Care is a relational ethic, grounded in the premise of interdependence.' She says that care is a human ethic, and that within a patriarchal framework, it provides a 'different voice' because 'it joins reason with emotion, mind with body, self with relationships, men with women, resisting the divisions that maintain a patriarchal order.' In *The Ethics of Care*, Fiona Robinson explains that, 'While households must make moral decisions about the organization of care, so, too, must communities and nation-states.' She says, 'Policy on care connects in fundamental ways with values and norms and the organization of society itself.'

When emotions are neglected, mental health issues can occur. These issues are often exacerbated, as a politics that does not come from love often does not recognise such problems when they arise, let alone provide a safe space within which they can be addressed. Short electoral cycles, although they bring some benefits, can frustrate long-term planning, as new governments can, and very often do, interrupt efforts at developing better systems. When it comes to health—mental, physical, and spiritual—the Politics of Love works to create a 'loving system' that wraps around people and nurtures the various dimensions of well-being. Healthcare should be 'affordable' and universal.

We believe that our political systems can and should operate much more sensitively than they currently do. Political decisions often cause anxiety. We worry about the impact of policies on our lives, and this has emotional consequences. It does not have to be this way. If people were confident that decisions were being made in love; that their fellow citizens were not only thinking about themselves, but about other people as well; and that their basic needs were not going to be compromised following any given election or public policy decision, this anxiety would be mitigated. But how can we ensure this?

We believe that what we need to do is nurture a culture of trust which is underpinned by reciprocity. This begins with our personal interactions—trusting and being trustworthy, as well as reciprocating and allowing other people to do the same, are things that all of us can do—but it must not stop there. Although it is impossible to legislate love, legislation can help to create the conditions within which love can flourish. Lynch, Baker, and Lyons write:

Societies cannot make anyone love anyone else, and to this extent the right to have loving, caring and solidary relationships is not directly enforceable. (Parents can be legally required to care for their children, but they cannot be forced to care about them.) But societies can work to establish the conditions in which these relationships can thrive.

They argue—and we agree—that equality is integral to this. We think that ensuring people's basic needs are met and establishing processes that protect us against their loss, are necessary, too. Under such conditions, loving values, such as *compassion, responsibility*, and *trust*, would achieve expression, and help us to further nurture one another.

The Politics of Love recognises that emotions can positively inform decision-making. It is also responsive to the emotional dimension of our lives. One of the dangers of thinking about politics in terms of emotion is that we risk legitimating thoughtless decision-making. For this reason, we believe that emotion must be tempered with intellect, reflection, and sensitivity—with, that is to say, wisdom. In this respect, the Politics of Love can be thought of as mature and considered, and as deeply concerned with everyone's well-being.

20

The Politics of Love

Where to from Here?

This article originally appeared on *Renegade Inc* in
August 2018.

There has recently been a resurgence of interest in love and
politics. We now regularly hear the word 'love' in activism and
political analysis. In the lead-up to the 2016 US Presidential
election, for example, a Love-Driven Politics Collective was
formed; and following the election of Donald Trump, Van
Jones mobilised a #LoveArmy. Alexandria Ocasio-Cortez
declared on Twitter, 'I practice a politics of love for all
people'; and most recently, Bishop Michael Curry explored
the concept in his royal wedding sermon on the power of love.

The idea that love might inform politics is not new. Martin
Luther King, Jr. famously invoked the power of love in his anti-
racist activism. In his sermon 'On Being a Good Neighbor',
which is collected in his book *Strength to Love*, he tells us that
our love ethic must incorporate 'universal altruism' if we are to
avoid what he calls 'the barbaric consequences of any tribal-
centered, national-centered, or racial-centered ethic.'

And some powerful contemporary thinkers have embraced the concept. In her book *All About Love*, bell hooks writes, 'All the great social movements for freedom and justice in our society have promoted a love ethic. . . . Were a love ethic informing all public policy in cities and towns, individuals would come together and map out programmes that would affect the good of everyone'. Feminists have explored related concepts in developing the ethics of care; and some philosophers and psychologists discuss 'affect', or the ways in which emotions are experienced, and its implications for politics.

But the term 'love' is, unfortunately, still very fragile. We have not yet done the necessary work to prepare it for the harsh world of politics. I first started writing about the Politics of Love with my good friend Max Harris in 2015. Since then, references to love in politics have increased remarkably. But love has still not established a place for itself in politics, and it is far from realising its full potential—as, that is, the foundation upon which our entire politics is built. I believe that the Politics of Love has this potential.

What is the Politics of Love? It is a values-based politics, which affirms the importance of people, and extends beyond us to non-human animals and the natural environment. It places love at the centre, and mobilises loving values, such as *understanding*, *respect*, and *trust*. It guides our political decisions; it also challenges us to re-think what counts as a 'political decision', and how we communicate with each other about important issues. The Politics of Love has precedents in the everyday acts of love we show to one another, as well as in the feminist, civil rights, and LGBTQI movements.

Its strength lies not only in love's power, but in the fact that almost all of us intuitively recognise its importance. 'Love' is a word that we all understand, and which brings us together.

But it is equally true that we have many different ideas about what love is, and that some of these conflict with each other. These competing accounts of love risk undermining the concept's capacity to positively inform politics. Just think about the different notions of love that attach to our ideas about family, romantic relationships, and God—and the potential that some of these concepts have to divide us! Love, in the political sense, is not, and cannot be, all that the word is currently used to mean; if it was, we would lose it in contradictions. We must engage critically with all of the impressions of love that we receive, and work toward an account of love that is actively inclusive, and that fulfils everyone's needs.

Max and I have explored different conceptions of love. He continues to favour the idea that love is 'a deep warmth that we direct towards other things', while I worry that the focus on 'other things' (including people) does not adequately accommodate self-love, and that the word 'warmth' does not capture the full range of expressions that love manifests. I have explored definitions such as 'love is for love, and, being love, is for people', and, 'to love is to want to be loving, to *work at* loving', which are, seemingly, circular, but which still, I believe, tell us something about what love is. It has also been helpful to think of love as 'a combination of care, concern, and commitment', although I worry that this represents an attempt to reduce the irreducible. I currently favour the idea that love is an orientation or 'attitude': that it is about how we engage in the world. Love is about how we relate: to ourselves, to each other, and to the world beyond us. It can be helpful to think of love as a value, but it is more than that: it determines and balances other values, like *humility* and *responsibility*. It guides us as we live our lives, and helps us decide how to act.

Many people are interested in the 'real-world implications' of the Politics of Love. Max and I have attempted to articulate some of these in a number of places. In our original article, for example, we suggested that the Politics of Love could lead to a renewed focus on rehabilitation in prisons worldwide,

> as an expression of the principle that warmth should be shown to all individuals, even those who have made mistakes, and of our understanding that individuals are never wholly responsible for their situations.

In his chapter on love and work in his book *The New Zealand Project*, Max proposes a universal basic income, a benefit paid to every member of a community regardless of their status of employment. Contrasting this with an insecure work benefit, the main aim of which is to get people into employment, he writes:

> A universal basic income best gives effect to a politics of love. It expresses confidence in people's ability to determine their own life courses, rather than demeaning or belittling them.

This, he argues, is equivalent to showing love to people. He says that a universal basic income could also enable people to leave abusive relationships by creating financial independence, allowing them to 'realise love more fully' in their own lives.

And in my article 'It Is Time to Imagine Our Entire Politics in Loving Terms', I argue that teaching indigenous languages such as te reo Māori in settler-colonial societies like our native Aotearoa New Zealand could promote *togetherness* and *understanding*, and that it might also support efforts at decolonisation. These are just examples of the proposals we have already made.

But what is more important, in my view, is how the Politics of Love operates, and what we can do to ensure that love, with all of its promise and potential, is enabled to inform politics. I don't pretend to have all of the answers. (Let me state for the record that I know that I don't!) As I've said before, the Politics of Love isn't a theory of, or belonging to, just one person, or even to two people; it actively seeks to involve all of us. I do have some suggestions, though, as to how we might realise love's radical political potential.

First, I think the Politics of Love needs to delimit itself. The competing definitions of love (and, to an extent, differing views about what it means for politics) threaten to undermine its power to motivate positive change. I think it's important that the Politics of Love promotes honest discussion and debate, but this doesn't mean that 'anything goes'. I conceive of the Politics of Love as a space within which people come together in good faith, with all of our diverse knowledges and histories, to do the serious work of making the world a better place for everyone who shares it.

I think of it as a round space, with love at its centre, and within which radical equality is the rule. We should nurture respectful exchange between diverse voices within this space. Importantly, it must include spokespeople for non-human animals and the natural environment—for, that is, those who are, and that which is, incapable of full self-representation. I follow bell hooks, who writes, in *Feminism Is for Everybody*, that 'there can be no love when there is domination', and so I understand the Politics of Love as anti-racist, anti-sexist, anti-speciesist, and opposed to all forms of domination; indeed, I understand this intersectional commitment as constituting the outer limits of this space.

Second, I think the Politics of Love needs to nurture unity within this space. It must invite all of those who are working for a better world into it; and we should strive, collaboratively, to ensure their continued inclusion within it. It is vitally important that we think through how this unity can be maintained, because it is on this that the strength of the Politics of Love depends. One way that we can do this is by centralising love, and ensuring that we continue to refer back to it when thinking and talking about politics. One point on which Max and I have disagreed is his description, or elaboration, of the Politics of Love as 'a politics of other people'. Although I agree that love asks us to look beyond ourselves, and that we should think about the implications that our decisions have for others, I worry that equating the Politics of Love with 'other people' diminishes the importance of self-love, and precludes love for non-human animals and the natural environment. By continually returning to 'love' and not getting diverted by lesser terms, we will ensure that the Politics of Love sustains its unifying potential. There is strength in unity: if we are going to realise a loving world, it will be by working together.

Third, I think the Politics of Love needs to cultivate a strong intellectual foundation. The biggest challenge that we face now consists in confronting the idea that love is too soft—too 'waffly', too 'airy-fairy'—for politics. Although the Politics of Love must remain accessible to all, and although it will be engaged with primarily outside of the academy, some of the intellectual 'grunt work' will, necessarily, be done within universities. Indeed, this work has already begun. Much of the work that has been, and is being, done on the ethics of care and 'affect', to return to those examples, could positively inform the Politics of Love.

It does seem to me, however, that most of those working in these, and related, areas are engaging all-too-tentatively with the notion of love. I suspect that they may be avoiding the word 'love'—consciously or otherwise—for fear of being ridiculed. (I worry, too, that by avoiding the term, they are often diverging from that which love suggests.) But if love is to achieve its potential, we must embrace the word itself—especially if the concept really is irreducible. Those in academia who are working within these spaces could unite around the Politics of Love. If they did, we would have a greater hope of achieving the world we are all trying to create.

As many of us are coming to appreciate, the Politics of Love has the potential to realise a better world. What it desperately needs now is for people to care. This is, really, the first requirement of the Politics of Love: that we care. As Rollo May states so clearly in his book *Love and Will*, 'Hate is not the opposite of love; apathy is.' We must now shake off our collective indifference, and engage in the difficult work that love requires of us.

Afterword

Whakautua te Kino

We are all heartbroken. Two days ago, on 15 March, there was a white supremacist terrorist attack in Christchurch, the third-largest city in Aotearoa New Zealand. This racist attack on two mosques has left 50 people dead; dozens more were injured, many of whom are still in Christchurch Hospital. All of us are grieving for our Muslim sisters and brothers.

I learnt of the attack while I was in Mezze Bar, working on the Politics of Love. The pain I felt while reading that news has not left me. As I write this, the book you are reading is being prepared for publication. There is still a lot that we don't know. For example, we don't yet know how many people were involved in the attack. It appears that there was one main attacker—but so far four people have been arrested in relation to it.

We are slowly learning about the victims. One of the first stories to emerge was that of Daoud Nabi, a 71-year-old Afghan refugee, who was the first person killed in the attack. He greeted the terrorist at the door to the mosque, saying, 'Welcome, brother.' (We know this, because the terrorist live-streamed his attack on Facebook.) The youngest victim is thought to be Mucad Ibrahim, a three-year-old boy, who went to the mosque with his older brother and father. In the coming days, their stories will be told. We mourn them all.

In her first public appearance following the attack, our prime minister, Jacinda Ardern, said that many of the victims were likely to be migrants who had chosen to make New Zealand home, and that some may even be refugees. Her message was clear: this *is* their home. 'They are us.' Ardern may not have chosen the right words, but she was correct in saying that our Muslim community is integral to Aotearoa New Zealand—*we are us*.

Unfortunately, Ardern's message didn't end there. 'The person who has perpetuated this violence against us is *not*,' she went on. 'They have no place in New Zealand.' Although the attacker has since been identified as an Australian citizen, it is not yet clear that no New Zealanders were involved. Ardern's comments are problematic, because they came dangerously close to suggesting that those who commit crimes should be deprived of their nationality— which is exactly what is happening to Shamima Begum, the British teenager who joined ISIS in Syria and is now being stripped of her citizenship. In my article 'Hijacked Emotions: Fighting Terrorism With Love', which I wrote in response to the terrorist attacks in Paris three years ago, and which is included in this book, I argued that our love must also extend to those who commit acts of terrorism—and I choose to reaffirm that today.

Ardern also described the attack as an 'unprecedented act of violence'—a statement which denies the violent reality of colonisation here in Aotearoa New Zealand. The New Zealand Wars, especially, provide many examples of racist violence. Māori remember this, even if our prime minister has forgotten. Her statement is symptomatic of the cultural amnesia that prevents us from critically discussing, and dismantling, racism.

It would be difficult to overstate the effect this tragedy has had on us as New Zealanders. The most seriously affected are our Muslim whānau, but all of us share in their shock and sadness. We are also angry. It is worth bearing in mind, especially if you haven't visited Aotearoa New Zealand, that we are a very small country—our population is around 4.8 million. This act of violence will continue to have a profound effect on us.

There have been signs of hope. Christchurch, or Ōtautahi, falls within the rohe (area) of my iwi, Ngāi Tahu. (I am not from Christchurch; my Māori ancestors are from the very bottom of the South Island and Stewart Island.) Following the attack, Lisa Tumahi, our Kaiwhakahaere (leader), made a statement, emphasising the importance of love:

Our priority is clear: aroha ki te tangata [love for people]. No matter how angry or scared we are feeling at the moment, we must come together as one strong community to show care and compassion for those who made Aotearoa their home and have now lost precious loved ones.

Although Prime Minister Jacinda Ardern's initial comments were problematic, she has shown admirable leadership over the last few days. Within twenty-four hours of the attack, she announced that semi-automatic weapons will soon be banned. It is worth asking why assault weapons were available for purchase in the first place, but it is important to remember that many nations have failed to secure gun-law reform following atrocities like this. The fact that Aotearoa New Zealand will have done so should serve as an example for the rest of the world.

Ardern has embodied New Zealanders' solidarity with the Muslim community. Following a phone call with Donald Trump, she reportedly said, 'He asked me what offer of support the United States could provide. My message was sympathy and love for all Muslim communities.' This is exactly what Ardern herself has shown: images of her wearing a hijab while meeting with members of our Muslim community have conveyed a powerful message of love not only to New Zealand Muslims, but to the Muslim world. This is the sort of leadership I expect of our politicians—and it is the sort of leadership you should expect of yours.

Yesterday afternoon, I attended a peace vigil in Aotea Square in Central Auckland, organised by the Khadija Leadership Network, an organisation which aims to build the capacity of Muslim women and encourage them to lead. This was a remarkable act of manaakitanga from members of our Muslim community, who, in spite of their grief, brought all of us together. Leaders from diverse communities and organisations spoke, and many emphasised the importance of love, saying that we must resist hatred and fear.

We heard from Muslim leaders, who expressed their pain, as well as their hope that we would come together in love. I was moved by their concern for our safety at the vigil, and I am grateful to them for patiently explaining to us what we should have understood all along: that they have not felt safe here, and that, although some of us were surprised that such an attack happened here, they had been anticipating and preparing for such an event.

I was especially heartened by the two speakers who attended from the Green Party of Aotearoa New Zealand: co-leader Marama Davidson (Ngāti Porou, Te Rarawa, Ngāpuhi), and Golriz Ghahraman, our first refugee MP. Davidson spoke of love, saying that one thing that needs to change in politics is the idea that we cannot be leaders and show vulnerability and emotion at the same time. She spoke of our mutuality:

Manaaki and tika, caring for each other in a way that is just and right, is what we should be upholding with every inch of ourselves. Upholding my mana, my dignity, is connected to upholding your mana, your dignity. I am as passionate about the well-being of your children as I am about making sure that my children are okay and have everything they need. These are the values that we should be demonstrating. . . .

She noted that many of our Muslim whānau are also Māori, helping us to forge connections between our indigenous and tauiwi communities; and she spoke to the intersectional nature of oppression:

> We will connect the dots so that people understand that all the oppressions that bring us down, for being gay, for being transgender, for being a person of colour, for being a woman in power—for being who we are—are connected and depend on each other to draw breath from the same oxygen that takes us all down.

She offered a different take on Ardern's 'they are us', saying, '[W]e will grieve, not just because you are one of us, but because *you are you*.' Ghahraman spoke to us about her own experiences as a woman of colour in power, and as a refugee in Aotearoa New Zealand, helping all of us to better understand the racism that assaults our society.

There is hope, too, in how we are talking to each other about this. Many of us here in Aotearoa New Zealand have received messages of love and support from our friends, family, and colleagues overseas, strengthening us, and validating the sorrow that we all feel. The language of love is being shared amongst New Zealanders. Among the whakataukī that are being used to express our wish to respond to Friday's attack with love is, *Whakautua te kino ki te pai, te riri ki te aroha.* ('Respond to evil with goodness, to anger with love.')

This gives me hope that, as Kiwis, we will work together to overcome hate, and realise love.

Unfortunately, over the last few days, the danger that we might *not* resist hatred has also become evident. Although messages of love have predominated, hateful, divisive rhetoric—celebrating Muslim deaths, or blaming Pākehā indiscriminately for the tragedy—has also circulated. It has been painful to witness a close friend sharing what I consider to be racist material on Facebook. While I agree with her that white New Zealanders must take responsibility for racism, the suggestion that all Pākehā are to blame for this attack ignores the anti-racist action that many Pākehā conscientiously engage in, and discourages loving dialogue. A better strategy, in my view, would be to explain why it is important that white New Zealanders resist racism, and to suggest practical ways in which we can do this.

One Australian senator has blamed the attack on immigration policies that 'allowed Muslim fanatics to migrate to New Zealand in the first place'. His horrendous words have been widely condemned, here and in Australia. In fact, his rhetoric was met by a 17-year-old boy, who is now being called 'Egg Boy' because he threw an egg at the politician while he was expressing his hateful views. The teenager was punched by the senator, twice, before being tackled and restrained by a number of men, one of whom kept him in a chokehold. While the boy's bravery and opposition to white supremacist rhetoric are being commended, we must recognise that his action was, in spite of this, physical assault, that this is a type of violence, and that, as such, it is—finally—inconsistent with the Politics of Love. (I have to admit: this is difficult to write, because it is so important that we oppose white supremacy. Nonetheless, I remain convinced that if love is to prevail, we must ensure that our discourse remains non-violent.) We should strive to embody the society we wish to live in.

As we might have expected, there have been calls not to 'politicise' the attack. The people who say this fail to understand that *almost everything* is political—including their insistence that we remain apolitical—and that theirs is a strategy used, consciously or otherwise, to avoid taking responsibility for racism. White supremacist terrorist attacks are inherently political; there is no 'non-political' way of responding to such acts.

Also concerning is the failure of Facebook and other digital platforms to promptly remove the live-stream footage of the terrorist attack. This is deeply disturbing: as well as showing a lack of respect for the victims, such videos have the potential to influence other would-be terrorists. Also very worryingly, a report today noted that, following the Prime Minister's announcement about our upcoming gun-law reform, sales of guns have increased significantly in what has been described as 'panic buying'. This is absolutely unacceptable. Guns will not make us safer—as the terrorist's actions prove.

Friday's white supremacist terrorist attack did not take place in isolation. Earlier this week, Green Party co-leader James Shaw—who, you will remember, declared, 'I'm proud to lead a party that stands for the politics of love and inclusion, not hate and fear'—was assaulted on his way to work in a politically motivated attack which left him with a black eye. Physical attacks on politicians are rare in Aotearoa New Zealand; only the Prime Minister and Deputy Prime Minister are routinely accompanied by security. It is important to note, however, that Green Party MPs—especially women of colour, such as Davidson and Ghahraman—are regularly subjected to sexist, racist threats of physical violence.

One thing that has gone largely uncommented-upon here is that March 15 was also the day of the School Strike for Climate, a worldwide protest led by students such as Greta Thunberg, a 16-year-old vegan activist from Sweden. Unlike the violence that we witnessed on Friday, this international youth movement for the environment *was* unprecedented: we have never seen such a large-scale youth movement for the environment. Due to the terrorist attack, however, it received very little coverage in Aotearoa New Zealand, and less coverage than it otherwise would have internationally. In light of this, Friday's terrorist attack should be viewed as a double tragedy: we desperately needed to hear the message that our children were delivering, and the fact that we didn't has serious implications for us all.

Auē, e kare mā! E tangi ana te ngākau. My heart is grieving for our Muslim brothers and sisters. I hope you know, e hoa mā, that, going forward, you will be able to depend on our love—that your fellow New Zealanders stand in solidarity with you. We are us!

The last few days have reaffirmed my faith in the profound importance of love. I have been inspired not only by words of love, but by many of the actions I have witnessed. And in everything that our response has lacked, I have recognised the need we have for a Politics of Love. This is urgent. It is time, now, for all of us who wish to realise love to work for it.

You'll be hearing from me. I hope to hear from you, too.

—17 March, 2019

Appendix

The Politics of Love

Taking the Project Forward

I presented this talk at The Politics of Love: A Conference, which Max Harris and I organised, at All Souls College, Oxford, on 15 December 2018.

Tēnā anō tātou katoa.

We want to begin by thanking all of you who have shared your thoughts so far today.

We now move into the stage of the conference that we have labelled 'Taking the Project Forward'. Soon, we will be breaking into groups, to further discuss the Politics of Love. We know you will all have plenty to share, and we're looking forward to finding out where these conversations lead! Shortly, Max will be offering some reflections on the presentations we have heard today, and suggesting questions to guide our discussions. Before that, though, I would like to share some of the thinking that we have done on the Politics of Love. We chose to share our views toward the end of the day because we wanted to give space to other thinkers, and because our thinking on the topic is still developing.

I should say that, although there is a lot of overlap in our thinking, Max and I do not agree on everything. If Max were to present our thoughts on the Politics of Love, he would likely emphasise different things. What follows, then, is my understanding of the Politics of Love, which is developing in relationship with Max's. We believe that disagreement can be constructive, and that the Politics of Love can accommodate diverse perspectives.

Max and I first sketched the Politics of Love in 2015, in an article which we published on Max's website, The Aotearoa Project. In that piece, we argued that politics can and should be more loving. It was, essentially, an expression of our belief that love can be both deeply critical and genuinely constructive. Since then, we have both spoken and written about the Politics of Love in a number of contexts and for a variety of publications.

The Politics of Love, as we understand it, is a values-based politics. It affirms the importance of people, and it extends beyond us to non-human animals and the natural environment. It holds that all people are important, and as such, it incorporates a commitment to radical equality. It is inclusive of non-human animals, because a politics that didn't take non-human animals, and their suffering, into account couldn't be considered 'loving'; and it encompasses a concern for the natural environment, recognising not only that it is important to our well-being, but that it is worthy of love in itself.

What is love? We think of love as an orientation or 'attitude'—or 'disposition', as Max prefers. It is a way of relating: to ourselves, to each other, and to the wider world.

The Politics of Love elaborates this 'attitude': it celebrates loving values, such as *care, concern*, and *commitment*, which can guide action and inform policy. These values are derived from, and held in balance by, love. How does love accomplish this? I imagine values as stars. All of these stars are always present, even if they aren't always visible. (It is worth remembering the Māori whakataukī: *He tini ngā whetū e ngaro i te kapua iti.* 'Many stars can be concealed by a small cloud.') And some, it is true, shine more brightly than others—*kindness, responsibility*, and *trust*, for example, outshine *anger* and *indignation*, but all have their place in the night sky. When, with open hearts, we look upwards for guidance, we are able to see what it is to love on any given night. The lover, then, is a stargazer, a constellation-maker; and what she sees is how to love.

Although love is generally thought of in emotional terms, we also view it as both critical and intellectual. While the Politics of Love recognises the importance of emotions—both the understanding that they bring, and that they form an integral part of who we are—it understands that feeling alone will not dismantle oppressive systems, like patriarchy, or enable us to decolonise our thinking. I believe that we must reject definitions of love that devalue intellectual engagement, including those that construe love only in emotional terms. We should affirm the value of intellectual commitment.

The idea that politics might be loving is not new. It has precedents in the everyday acts of love we show to one another, as well as in the feminist, civil rights, and LGBTQI movements. Martin Luther King, Jr., for example, famously invoked love in his anti-racist activism. In his sermon 'Loving

Your Enemies', which is collected in the book *Strength to Love*, he says, 'There will be no permanent solution to the race problem until oppressed men develop the capacity to love their enemies.' As African American theorist bell hooks writes in her book *All About Love*, 'All the great social movements for freedom and justice in our society have promoted a love ethic.' When Max and I think about historical examples of loving politics, we remember the passive resistance at Parihaka in Aotearoa New Zealand. The prophet Te Whiti o Rongomai—with his whanaunga Tohu Kākahi—led the people in passive resistance against the unjust confiscation of their land. Te Whiti instructed them to plough land that had been taken from them, erect fences, and remove surveyor's pegs. In urging the people of Parihaka to resist injustice but insisting that they do so peacefully, Te Whiti demonstrated the basis upon which our peoples might live together in the future.

The Politics of Love is an actively inclusive framework. I imagine it as a round space, with love at its centre, and within which mutuality guides exchange. We affirm bell hooks' sclaim, which she makes in *Feminism Is for Everybody*, that 'there can be no love when there is domination'—and so, we understand the Politics of Love as anti-racist, anti-sexist, anti-speciesist, and opposed to all forms of domination. Indeed, I think of this intersectional commitment as constituting the outer limits of this space. We should work to nurture respectful exchange between diverse voices within this space. Importantly, the Politics of Love must involve spokespeople for non-human animals and the natural environment—for those who are, and that which is, incapable of full self-representation. This 'space' extends both inwards and outwards; it is an ethic that we can embody, as individuals and as communities; and it is through relationship that this space is realised. We see an affinity with what angel Kyodo williams has termed 'radical dharma'. She writes:

> Each community possesses, as Gandhi offered, a piece of the truth, of Dharma. When we seek the embodiment of these truths, giving ourselves permission to be more honest, more healed, more whole, more complete—when we become radical—neither the path of solely inward-looking liberation nor the pursuit of an externalised social liberation prevails; rather a third space, as-yet-unknown, emerges. It is a radical dharma. And it is ours.

Within this space, people come together to deliberate—and it is from this space that we act. As important as the ideas that inform this politics, and the actions that it leads to, is how we talk to each other about politics. We need to eschew the pettiness—the bickering, the name-calling—that has come to characterise modern politics. Instead, values such as *humility*, *listening*, and *understanding* should guide political exchange. We believe that it is through loving exchange that we will develop genuine and lasting solutions to our problems. In this way, then, the Politics of Love incorporates dialogue, theory, and action. (This is not to say that agonism and conflict have no place in politics—simply that these must be underpinned by love. Very often, confrontation is needed to develop loving communities.) We tend to have rigid ideas about what political action involves, but the Politics of Love manifests in a diverse variety of actions, all of which are guided by love. Persuasion, example-setting, voluntary work, employment, protesting, campaigning, voting, and public service—as well as many other types of action—can all be utilised in expressing loving politics.

Importantly, the Politics of Love is engaged in creating solutions. In our writing, Max and I have attempted to illustrate what loving politics might look like in practice. I want to share some examples here—not because I believe that Max and I have all the answers (we don't), but because I think that if any of us are going to claim that love can inform politics, and if we want this claim to be taken seriously, we need to be able to say how it might do so.

In our original article for The Aotearoa Project, Max and I suggested that the Politics of Love could lead to a renewed focus on rehabilitation in prisons, as an expression of the principle that warmth should be shown to all people, even those who have made mistakes, and of our understanding that individuals are never wholly responsible for their situations.

As another example: in the chapter on love and work in his book *The New Zealand Project*, Max proposed a universal basic income, a benefit paid to every member of a community regardless of their status of employment. Contrasting this with an insecure work benefit, the main aim of which is to get people into employment, he writes:

A universal basic income best gives effect to a politics of love. It expresses confidence in people's ability to determine their own life courses, rather than demeaning or belittling them.

This, he argues, is equivalent to showing love to people. He says that a universal basic income could also enable people to leave abusive relationships by creating financial independence, allowing them to 'realise love more fully' in their own lives.

And in a chapter for *The Interregnum*, Max argues that love might start to address 'the epidemic of loneliness that is faced by young people, the elderly, those with mental health difficulties, some of those who are unemployed, many of those who are incarcerated, and perhaps all those who are excluded from society.' He writes:

The mere expression of a politics of love could hearten those who feel lonely; it could send a message to them that they are not alone and not ignored. Policies flowing from the politics of love—which could include renewed support for prisoner rehabilitation and refugee resettlement programmes, increased investment in sport and general community organisations, and the strengthening of services such as Lifeline and the Samaritans—might address loneliness even more directly. Put simply: love, and a politics of love, could be the answer—or part of the answer—to loneliness.

In my writing, I have argued that the Māori concept of aroha, which is usually translated as 'love', can help us to reconceptualise, and address, racism. In my article 'The Thin Line Between Dickishness and Casual Racism'—I didn't give it that title!—I wrote:

> Aroha helps us to see that racism isn't someone else's problem: it's our problem. When we love each other— when we care about other people—we're hurt by what hurts them, and we celebrate what benefits them, even if we don't know them personally. Aroha is the answer not because love will give us an easy fix, but because it repositions us relative to our concerns. It encourages us to see racism as our problem, and urges us to resist it. Aroha requires us to take this one step further, though: it asks that we give each other opportunities to learn, to grow, and to move beyond our mistakes.

And Mexican philosopher Carla Alicia Suárez Félix and I recently argued that the Politics of Love, with its intersectional commitment to anti-speciesism, leads us toward veganism— while heeding the caution of ecofeminists, such as Lori Gruen, who writes:

> Though most of us can readily eschew animal parts in our own diets, ecofeminists are mindful of the violence perpetuated in many gendered, racialized, and colonial contexts as well as the realities of a changing climate and thus forgo top-down, absolute universalizing judg-

ments that everyone, everywhere should see "veganism as a moral baseline." Instead, most ecofeminists argue for "contextual moral veganism" that recognizes both the moral centrality of a vegan diet and contextual exigencies that impede one's ability to live without directly killing or using others.

... as well as the wisdom of Zen master Thích Nhất Hạnh, who reminds us that when we make mistakes, it is usually because we are unskillful, and not because we want to do harm.

'Love' is becoming increasingly popular. In Aotearoa New Zealand's most recent general election, the Green Party campaigned on love, with co-leader James Shaw declaring, 'I'm proud to lead a party that stands for the politics of love and inclusion, not hate and fear.' When it formed a coalition with the Labour Party, Prime Minister Jacinda Ardern announced that her government would be 'empathetic'. In Australia, MP Andrew Leigh has spoken extensively on the Politics of Love. And in the United States, a #LoveArmy, led by Van Jones, was formed following the election of Donald Trump; the fiftieth anniversary of the assassination of Dr. King led to a renewed discussion of his ideas of civic love; and last year, Alexandria Ocasio-Cortez, who was recently elected to congress, tweeted, 'I practice a politics of love for all people'. Here in the United Kingdom, Bishop Michael Curry explored the concept in his widely-reported-on royal wedding sermon on the power of love.

However, the idea that love should inform politics has also been criticised. For example, it has been said that love is too weak a concept for the hard world of politics. Another criticism is that the word 'love' is too vague—too waffly, too airy-fairy—to give us any real guidance, and that it can be used to mean anything we want it to. There are many more. (Including my favourite, made in response to an article I wrote for the *Guardian*: someone commented that I'd been watching too much *Star Trek*! . . . which—yes, okay, I admit it—is probably true.) We take (most of) these criticisms seriously, and we believe that those of us who want to see the Politics of Love succeed must engage with them. In light of these criticisms, we believe that, at this point in time, the Politics of Love needs three things:

First, we think the Politics of Love needs to delimit itself. The competing definitions of love (and, to an extent, differing views about what it means for politics) threaten to undermine its power to motivate positive change. It is vitally important that the Politics of Love promotes honest discussion and debate—but this doesn't mean that 'anything goes'. 'Love' does not, and cannot, mean everything that the word is taken to mean—at least not for politics. We must strive for greater clarity around what 'love' is, and what it means for politics.

Second, the Politics of Love needs to nurture unity. It must invite all of those who are working for a better world into its space; and we should strive, collectively, to ensure their continued inclusion within it. It is vitally important that we think through how unity can be maintained—because it is on this that the strength of the Politics of Love depends. One way that we might do this is by centralising love, and ensuring that we continue to refer back to it when thinking and talking about politics. The word 'love' has power—most of us recognise its weight—and, importantly, it can give us guidance. If we continue to return to the word 'love', we will ensure that the Politics of Love sustains its unifying potential. There is strength in unity: if we are going to realise a loving world, it will be by working together.

Third, the Politics of Love needs a strong intellectual foundation. The idea that 'love' is too soft for politics is one that we must confront: we must show that it is not. Although the Politics of Love must remain accessible to all, and although it will be engaged with, primarily, *outside* of the academy, some of this intellectual 'grunt work' will, necessarily, be done within universities. It is partly for this reason that we have organised this conference. Indeed, this academic work has already begun: much of the work that has been, and is being, done on the ethics of care and 'affect', to give only two examples, could positively inform the Politics of Love. (It does seem to me, however, that most of those working in these, and related, areas are engaging all-too-tentatively with the notion of love. I suspect that they may be avoiding the word 'love'—consciously or otherwise—for fear of being ridiculed. I worry, too, that by avoiding the term, they are often diverging from that which love suggests.) But if love is to realise its potential, we must embrace the word itself. Our hope is that those in academia who are working within these spaces will unite around the Politics of Love. If they do, we have a much greater hope of achieving the world we are all trying to create.

Before I hand over to Max, I would like to share one more thought. Many people are reluctant to speak up for strong ideals such as love because they recognise that they themselves are imperfect. This is something that Max and I have discussed at length in our personal conversations. Who are we to talk about love? We can both recall times when we have said and done things that are unloving. Neither of us comes close to embodying 'perfect love'. While we believe that this understanding should move us toward humility, we do not think that it should prevent anyone from trying to make the world a better place. (If all of us drew that conclusion, who would be left to do the work of love?) It takes courage, I think, to speak up for an ideal; but it is a powerful act. When we affirm love, we teach each other that it is okay to work in love. It is vitally important that we do this, because love needs all of us thinking, feeling, and acting. To love is—at least in part—to continuously strive to transcend one's imperfections, and to actively allow other people to do the same.

He aroha whakatō, he aroha puta mai. If love is sown, then love will grow.

Glossary

Many Māori words and sayings have multiple meanings, which vary according to context. The meanings offered here relate specifically to how the words and sayings are used in this collection.

Aotearoa	New Zealand
aroha	love
arohatia te reo	love the [Māori] language
he tōrangapū aroha	a loving politics
hoa ako	fellow learners
hui	gathering, get-together
iwi	tribe
Kāi Tahu	a Māori tribe (also *Ngāi Tahu*)
Kāi Tahutaka	Kāi Tahu culture, Kāi Tahu-ness
kaupapa	issue, initiative
kupu	word/s
Māori	indigenous to New Zealand, indigenous New Zealander/s, of New Zealand's indigenous culture

mita	dialect, cadence
Ngāi Tahu	a Māori tribe (also *Kāi Tahu*)
Pākehā	New Zealand European
pou	post, pillar
rangatahi	youth, young people
rangatiratanga	leadership, sovereignty
reo	language
tamariki	children
tāngata	people
taonga	treasure, valued possession
tauiwi	non-Māori people
te ao Māori	the Māori world
Te Marautanga o Aotearoa	the Māori-medium curriculum
te reo	the [Māori] language
te reo Māori	the Māori language
te reo Pākehā	the English language
te reo rangatira	the chiefly [Māori] language
Te Tiriti o Waitangi	the Māori-language version of The Treaty of Waitangi
Te Waipounamu	the South Island of New Zealand
tohunga reo	[Māori] language expert
tumuaki	leader of an organisation
wānanga	educational forum
whakaaro	ideas, thinking
whakapapa	to relate to through ancestry
whakataukī	traditional saying

whakatauākī	traditional saying
whakawhanaungatanga	relationship building
whanaunga	relation

<u>Whakataukī, whakatauākī</u>

Aroha mai, aroha atu.	Let's show our love.
He aroha whakatō,	If love is sown, then love
he aroha puta mai.	will grow.
He iwi kotahi tātou.	We are [now] one people.
He tini ngā whetū e	Many stars can be concealed
ngaro i te kapua iti.	by a small cloud.

Select Bibliography

Adams, Carol J. "What Came Before *The Sexual Politics of Meat*: The Activist Roots of a Critical Theory." In *Species Matters: Humane Advocacy and Cultural Theory*, edited by Marianne DeKoven and Michael Lundblad, 103–138 (New York: Columbia University Press, 2012).

Adams, Carol J., and Lori Gruen, eds. *Ecofeminism: Feminist Intersections with Other Animals and the Earth* (New York: Bloomsbury, 2014).

Anapol, Deborah. *Polyamory in the 21st Century: Love and Intimacy with Multiple Partners* (Lanham, Md.: Rowman & Littlefield, 2010).

Armstrong, Dave. "Compulsory English in Schools." *PPTA News: The Magazine of New Zealand Secondary Teachers* 38, no. 1 (2017): 17.

Baldwin, James. *The Fire Next Time* (New York: The Dial Press, 1963).

Barlow, Cleve. *Tikanga Whakaaro: Key Concepts in Māori Culture* (Melbourne: Oxford University Press, 1991).

Bentham, Jeremy. *An Introduction to the Principles of Morals and Legislation* (Oxford: Oxford University Press, 1907).

Camus, Albert. *The Myth of Sisyphus*. Translated by Justin O'Brien (London: Hamish Hamilton, 1955).

——. *Notebooks 1942–1951*. Translated by Justin O'Brien. (Chicago: Ivan R. Dee, 2010).

——. *The Rebel*. Translated by Anthony Bower (London: Hamish Hamilton, 1953).

Chapple, Christopher. "Inherent Value without Nostalgia: Animals and the Jaina Tradition." In *A Communion of Subjects: Animals in Religion, Science, and Ethics*, edited by Paul Waldau and Kimberley Patton, 241–249 (New York: Columbia University Press, 2006).

Coates, Ta-Nehisi. *Between the World and Me* (New York: Spiegel & Grau, 2015).

——. "The Enduring Solidarity of Whiteness." *The Atlantic*, 2016. <https://www.theatlantic.com/politics/archive/2016/02/why-we-write/459909/>.

Compassion in World Farming. *Strategic Plan 2013–2017: For Kinder, Fairer Farming Worldwide* (Godalming, Surrey: Compassion in World Farming, 2013) <https://www.ciwf.org.uk/media/3640540/ciwf_strategic_plan_20132017.pdf>.

Faria, Catia. "Lo personal es político: feminismo y antiespecismo." *Revista Latinoamericana de Estudios Críticos Animales* 2 (2017): 18–38.

Foer, Jonathan Safran. *Eating Animals* (New York: Little, Brown and Company, 2009).

Frankfurt, Harry G. *The Reasons of Love* (Princeton, NJ: Princeton University Press, 2004).

Friedman, Marilyn. "Feminism in Eethics: Conceptions of Autonomy." In *The Cambridge Companion to Feminism in Philosophy*, edited by Miranda Fricker and Jennifer Hornsby, 205–224 (Cambridge: Cambridge University Press, 2000).

Fromm, Erich. *The Art of Loving* (New York: HarperCollins, 2006).

Gandhi, Mohandas K. *Gandhi's Health Guide* (Freedom, CA: The Crossing Press, 2000).

——. *Hind Swaraj or Indian Home Rule*. Rev. ed. (Ahmedabad: Navajivan Press, 1939).

Gilligan, Carol. *Joining the Resistance* (Cambridge: Polity Press, 2011).

Gruen, Lori. *Entangled Empathy: An Alternative Ethic for Our Relationships with Animals* (New York: Lantern Books, 2015).

——. "Facing Death and Practicing Grief." In *Ecofeminism: Feminist Intersections with Other Animals and the Earth*, edited by Carol J. Adams and Lori Gruen, 127–141 (New York: Bloomsbury, 2014).

Hanisch, Carol. "The Personal Is Political." In *Notes from the Second Year: Women's Liberation: Major Writings of the Radical Feminists*, edited by Shulamith Firestone and Anne Koedt, 76–78 (New York: Radical Feminism, 1970).

Harré, Niki. *Psychology for a Better World: Strategies to Inspire Sustainability* (Auckland: Auckland University Press, 2011).

Harris, Max. "A Crazy Little Thing Called Tax." *The Spinoff*, 2018 <https://thespinoff.co.nz/business/04-04-2018/crazy-little-thing-called-tax/>.

——. "Join the Party of Love." *Aeon*, 2017 <https://aeon.co/essays/it-is-time-for-love-to-become-a-radical-force-in-politics>.

——. *The New Zealand Project* (Wellington: Bridget Williams Books, 2017).

——. "The Politics of Love—In An Age of Loneliness." In *The Interregnum: Rethinking New Zealand*, edited by Morgan Godfery, 141–153 (Wellington: Bridget Williams Books, 2016).

——. "A Radical Party of Love." *Medium*, 2016 <https://medium.com/perspectiva-institute/a-radical-politics-of-love-fbe259170646>.

Harris, Max and Philip McKibbin. "The Politics of Love." *The Aotearoa Project*, 2015 <https://theaotearoaproject.wordpress.com/2015/05/20/the-politics-of-love-max-harris-and-philip-mckibbin/>.

hooks, bell. *All About Love: New Visions* (New York: William Morrow, 2000).

——. *Communion: The Female Search for Love* (New York: William Morrow, 2002).

——. *Feminism Is for Everybody* (London: Pluto Press, 2000).

——. *Feminist Theory: From Margin to Center*. 2nd ed. (London: Pluto Press, 2000).

———. *Salvation: Black People and Love* (New York: William
    Morrow, 2001).

———. *The Will to Change: Men, Masculinity, and Love* (New York:
    Washington Square Press, 2004).

Hoskins, Te Kawehau and Alison Jones, eds. *The New Zealand
    Journal of Educational Studies, Te Hautaki Mātai Mātauranga
    o Aoatearoa, Special Issue: He Aha te Kaupapa? Critical
    Conversations in Kaupapa Māori* (Christchurch: New
    Zealand Association for Research in Education, 2012).

Jamieson, Dale. "Loving Nature." World Philosophy Day Lecture,
    NC State University, November 16, 2017.

Judt, Tony. *Ill Fares the Land: A Treatise On Our Present Discontents*
    (London: Penguin Books, 2010).

King, Jr., Martin Luther. *Strength to Love* (Minneapolis, MN:
    Fortress Press, 2010).

———. *Where Do We Go from Here: Chaos or Community?* (Boston,
    MA: Beacon Press, 2010).

Leigh, Andrew. "The Politics of Love." Speech presented in
    Melbourne, Australia, August 16, 2016 <http://www.
    andrewleigh.com/the_politics_of_love_speech>.

Lynch, Kathleen, John Baker, and Maureen Lyons. *Affective
    Equality: Love, Care, and Injustice* (Basingstoke, Hampshire,
    UK: Palgrave Macmillan, 2009).

Lyons, Oren. "An Iroquois Perspective." In *American Indian
    Environments: Ecological Issues in Native American History*,
    edited by Christopher Vecsey and Robert W. Venables,
    171–174 (New York: Syracuse University Press, 1980).

Mahâvîra. "Âkârâṅga Sûtra." In *Jaina Sūtras: Part I*, translated by
    Hermann Jacobi, 1–213 (Delhi, India: Motilal Banarsidass,
    1964).

May, Rollo. *Love and Will* (New York: W. W. Norton &
    Company, 1969).

McIntosh, Peggy. *White Privilege and Male Privilege: A Personal
    Account of Coming to See Correspondences through Work in
    Women's Studies* (Wellesley, MA: Wellesley Centers for
    Women, 1988).

Ministry of Education. *The New Zealand Curriculum* (Wellington: Ministry of Education, 2015).

Moon, Paul. *Ka Ngaro Te Reo: Māori Language Under Siege in the Nineteenth Century* (Dunedin: Otago University Press, 2016).

Nagel, Thomas. "What Is It Like to Be a Bat?" *The Philosophical Review* 83, no. 4 (1974): 435–50.

Nhất Hạnh, Thích. *How to Love* (Berkeley, CA: Parallax Press, 2015).

Nussbaum, Martha C. *Women and Human Development: The Capabilities Approach* (New York: Cambridge University Press, 2000).

Oppenlander, Richard A. "Our Lifeline Revealed Through the Eye of Justice." In *Circles of Compassion: Essays Connecting Issues of Justice*, edited by Will Tuttle, 171–181 (Danvers, MA: Vegan Publishers, 2014).

Proctor, Helen. "Animal Sentience: Where Are We and Where Are We Heading?" *Animals* 2, no. 4 (2012): 628–39.

Rawls, John. *A Theory of Justice* (Cambridge, MA: Harvard University Press, 1999).

Rilke, Rainer Maria. *Rilke on Love and Other Difficulties: Translations and Considerations of Rainer Maria Rilke*. Edited and translated by John J. L. Mood (New York: W. W. Norton & Company, 1975).

Robinson, Fiona. *The Ethics of Care: A Feminist Approach to Human Security* (Philadelphia, PA: Temple University Press, 2011).

Scott, Dick. *Ask That Mountain: The Story of Parihaka* (Auckland: Southern Cross, 1975).

Shaw, James. "Speech to the Federation of Multicultural Councils AGM." Presented in Dunedin, July 1, 2017 <https://www.greens.org.nz/news/press-release/speech-federation-multicultural-councils-agm>.

Singer, Peter. *Animal Liberation*. Rev. ed. (New York: HarperCollins, 2009).

Smith, Linda Tuhiwai. *Decolonizing Methodologies: Research and Indigenous Peoples*. 2nd ed. (London: Zed Books, 2012).

Spiegel, Marjorie. *The Dreaded Comparison: Human and Animal Slavery* (London: Heretic Books, 1988).

Srinivasan, Amia. "The Sucker, the Sucker!" *London Review of Books* 39, no. 17 (2017): 23–25. <https://www.lrb.co.uk/v39/n17/amia-srinivasan/the-sucker-the-sucker>.

Stallwood, Kim. *Growl: Life Lessons, Hard Truths, and Bold Strategies from an Animal Advocate* (New York: Lantern Books, 2014).

Standing, Guy. *The Precariat: The New Dangerous Class* (London: Bloomsbury, 2011).

Te Tāhuhu o te Mātauranga. *Te Marautanga o Aotearoa* (Te Whanganui-a-Tara: Te Tāhuhu o te Mātauranga, 2017).

Te Wāhanga, Jessica Hutchings, Helen Potter, and Katrina Taupo, eds. *Kei Tua o te Pae Hui Proceedings: The Challenges of Kaupapa Māori in the 21st Century* (Wellington: New Zealand Council for Educational Research, 2011).

"The New Testament." In *Good News Bible*. Rev. ed. (Sydney: Bible Society, 1994).

Tuttle, Will, ed. *Circles of Compassion: Essays Connecting Issues of Justice* (Danvers, MA: Vegan Publishers, 2014).

United Nations Environment Programme. *Assessing the Environmental Impacts of Consumption and Production: Priority Products and Materials* (New York: United Nations, 2010).

Walker, Alice. "Preface." In *The Dreaded Comparison: Human and Animal Slavery*, by Marjorie Spiegel, 9–10 (London: Heretic Books, 1988).

Wiley, Kristi. "Five-Sensed Animals in Jainism." In *A Communion of Subjects: Animals in Religion, Science, and Ethics*, edited by Paul Waldau and Kimberley Patton, 250–255 (New York: Columbia University Press, 2006).

williams, angel Kyodo, Lama Rod Owens, and Jasmine Syedullah. *Radical Dharma: Talking Race, Love and Liberation* (Berkeley, CA: North Atlantic Books, 2016).

Acknowledgements

Many people helped shape the pieces in this collection. *Ehara taku toa i te toa takitahi, engari he toa takitini.* Thank you to Max Harris, for first thinking through the Politics of Love with me, and for your work co-organising The Politics of Love: A Conference. Thank you, also, to Sarah Illingworth, Carla Alicia Suárez Félix, and Julie Timmins, for exploring this vision with me in writing. I am grateful to the many thinkers whose work on love has influenced my own, foremost among whom are bell hooks, Martin Luther King, Jr., and Thích Nhất Hạnh. Thank you to those of you who have discussed the Politics of Love with me, including, especially, Simon Waigth, Danielle Duffield, and Natasha Oliver. Thank you to Nik Parkin, for your helpful comments on a draft of the introduction to this book. Thank you, also, to Martin Rowe, for your support of this project, and to the rest of the team at Lantern Books, for your work in bringing this book to publication. To Shane Hansen, ngā mihi nui ki a koe for allowing me to use your art on the cover—your work speaks with gentle understanding to our vulnerability, reminding us of what is important, and helping us to appreciate the vibrancy of which we are part.

I am extremely grateful to those of you who supported the PledgeMe campaign, enabling me to attend the Minding Animals International Conference in Mexico in 2018. I would also like to acknowledge the sustaining support of Ben Allen, Emma Thompson, and Brendon Marshall. To those of you whose love nourishes my own, especially Gran, Rauhina Scott-Fyfe, Shane Smits, Max Harris, Carla Alicia Suárez Félix, Beca Gaelic, Julie Timmins, and Joanne McNaughton, taku aroha ki a koutou. Finally, thank you to the staff at Mezze Bar, for your hospitality during the long hours I spent working on these pieces.

Contributors

Max Harris is an Examination Fellow at All Souls College, Oxford. Originally from Aotearoa New Zealand, he is the author of *The New Zealand Project* (Bridget Williams Books, 2017) and has written about various topics in progressive politics for outlets such as *Aeon*, *Novara Media*, and *openDemocracy*. He has also taken part in campaigning and activist projects, including in the fields of criminal justice and decolonisation. In 2018, he and Philip McKibbin organised The Politics of Love: A Conference at All Souls College, Oxford.

Sarah Illingworth is a media and communications practitioner from Auckland, New Zealand. She launched and ran Impolitikal, an online zine with a social, political focus between 2014 and 2018. She co-edited *Don't Dream It's Over: Reimagining Journalism in Aotearoa New Zealand* (Freerange Press, 2016). In a past life she interviewed celebrities like Lady Gaga, Steven Spielberg, and Yoko Ono, and wrote encouraging content for a website for teenage girls. She has a Master of Science in Poverty and Development from The University of Manchester's Global Development Institute.

Carla Alicia Suárez Félix is a Mexican philosopher and activist. She is the organiser of the Circle of Antispeciesist Studies in Querétaro, and she works on the following topics: speciesism, animal exploitation, bioethics, feminism, ecofeminism, and ethics.

Julie Timmins was a founder of Child Poverty Action Group (CPAG) in Aotearoa New Zealand and continues to work in the area of social justice. She has been involved in several research publications for CPAG, worked on the Family 100 project for the Auckland City Mission, and is a Trustee of Ngā Tāngata Microfinance Trust. She has a Master of Science in Equality Studies from University College Dublin.

About the Author

Photo: Viktória Lencsés

PHILIP MCKIBBIN is a writer from Aotearoa New Zealand. He is of Pākehā (New Zealand European) and Māori (Ngāi Tahu) descent. He has written for the *Guardian*, *Renegade Inc*, and *Takahē*. He holds a Master of Arts in Philosophy from The University of Auckland, and a Diploma in Te Pīnakitanga ki te Reo Kairangi (Māori Language Excellence) from Te Wānanga o Aotearoa. He first wrote about the Politics of Love in 2015, with his friend and fellow New Zealander Max Harris. In 2018, they hosted The Politics of Love: A Conference at All Souls College, Oxford. www.philip-mckibbin.com

About the Artist

Photo: Renee Lansdowne

SHANE HANSEN is an artist, a designer of graphics, furniture, and fashion, a loving husband, and doting dad to two gorgeous boys. Born in New Zealand in the 1970s, he is of Māori (Tainui, Ngāti Māhanga, Ngāti Hine), Chinese, Danish, and Scottish descent. Aotearoa is in his blood, in his heart, and in his art. Shane's creations spring from the characters, creatures, moods, memories, and moments lying deep within the country he calls home. His artistic world is one of bold colours, modern Māori motifs, optimism and clarity inspired by his multicultural heritage, and an admiration for pop art, strong graphics, and a profound appreciation of the landscapes that surround him. As well as depicting the various shapes and tones of Aotearoa, Shane's works represent ideas about who he is, where he comes from, and how he fits into the country he grew up in. His work has become a channel for an ongoing examination of his multicultural heritage, and he is determined to continue pushing the parameters of what he can express and achieve through it. www.shanehansen.co.nz

About the Publisher

LANTERN BOOKS was founded in 1999 on the principle of living with a greater depth and commitment to the preservation of the natural world. In addition to publishing books on animal advocacy, veganism, religion, and environmentalism, Lantern is dedicated to printing books in the United States on recycled paper and saving resources in day-to-day operations. Lantern is honored to be a recipient of the highest standard in environmentally responsible publishing from the Green Press Initiative.